To Have and To Hold

101 Smart Strategies to Engage Your Employees

By Lisa Ryan

Other Books by Lisa Ryan

Manufacturing Engagement:
98 Proven Strategies to Attract and Retain Your Industry's Top Talent

The Upside of Down Times:
Discovering the Power of Gratitude

From Afraid to Speak to Paid to Speak:
How Overcoming Public Speaking Anxiety Boosts Your Confidence and Career

The Verbal Hug:
101 Absolutely Awesome Ways to Express Appreciation

Express Gratitude, Experience Good:
A Daily Gratitude Journal

Thank You Notes:
Your 30-Days of Gratitude Workbook

52 Weeks of Gratitude:
Transformation Through Appreciation

52 More Week of Gratitude:
Thank Your Way to Happiness

To Have and To Hold

101 Smart Strategies to Engage Your Employees

To Have and To Hold

101 Smart Strategies to Engage Employees

By Lisa Ryan

Published by Grategy® Press

Cleveland, Ohio

Grategy, LLC

3222 Perl Ct.

North Royalton, OH 44133

216-359-1134

lisa@grategy.com

www.grategy.com

www.LisaRyanSpeaks.com

To my wonderful husband, Scott. On April 13, 1996, we took our vows "to have and to hold" each other. Each day with you is a blessing and I am grateful for US!

It's never too early or too often

To let others know you appreciate them.

~ Lisa Ryan

Table of Contents

PART 1

To have and to hold

Gratitude is to the workplace as oil is to an engine. It needs to be applied liberally and throughout and is of such importance, that a fresh supply must be added regularly to ensure success and longevity. ~ Adapted from a quote by Matthew Smith

Catch your employees doing their job well.

A program participant shared, "When I do something wrong, I get recognized 100% of the time. When I do something well, I rarely get noticed." This is not uncommon. Studies show that only 42% of employees received positive feedback from their manager in the past twelve months. Just like receiving so little positive feedback will kill a personal relationship, it's just as detrimental in the workplace.

Dr. John Gottman, a marriage researcher, discovered that in marriages that endure, there is a 5:1 positivity ratio. This means that for each negative comment a partner says to the other, he or she must say five positive things to make up for it.

Marcial Losada took that same premise into the workplace. He found a 6:1 ratio for high-performing teams, 3:1 for average performing teams, and 3:1 for low-performing teams. Low-performing team members hear three times as many negatives as positives. It's a reminder of the old saying, "The beatings will continue until morale improves." It doesn't work.

Action Ideas:

1. When you see an employee doing something well, give immediate positive feedback.

2. Encourage peer-to-peer recognition. Make it fun to give credit to each other.

3. Stop trying to fix what's broken. Focus on your employees' strengths and help them make the things they do well even better.

Regularly thank your staff.

Vow to let your staff know that you appreciate them as both people and as producers. Be sincere. Your employees can tell when you're not.

Ken Blanchard of One-Minute Manager fame said, "Effective praising has to be specific. Just walking around saying 'thanks for everything' is meaningless. If you say, 'great job' to a poor performer and the same thing to a good performer, you'll sound ridiculous to the poor performer and will demotivate the good performer."

Express your gratitude in the way your employees like to receive it. Some people like public recognition, others abhor it. Sometimes a one-on-one conversation or a handwritten note is much more appreciated than making a big deal out of the employee's success. Pay attention and get to know how your employees are "wired" when it comes to accepting thanks.

Action Ideas:

1. Say "thank you" early and often. When you hear a "thank you" from someone else, instead of saying "No problem" or "It was nothing," say, "You're welcome" or "My pleasure." In responding positively, you'll complete the cycle of appreciation.

2. Keep a log of your employees' successes. In doing so, your list will also make performance reviews easier and more pleasant.

3. Don't wait for someone to have to "go above and beyond" to recognize them. When someone is doing better than THEY normally do, make sure to acknowledge them based on their past actions.

Understand the "why."

Employees are more likely to commit to your company when they understand the role they play in your business's mission and long-term aspirations. Where there is confusion, indifference, or a lack of purpose in crafting big picture goals, your staff may become disengaged.

Take a moment and figure out what difference your product or service makes in the world. How do you serve? Whom do you support? Ask employees for their ideas as well.

Here's an example of importance of having a mission.

A man asked three bricklayers what they did for a living. The first replied, "I'm laying bricks." The second answered, "I'm putting up a wall." The third responded with pride in his voice, "I'm building a cathedral."

Food for thought: are your employees laying bricks, putting up walls, or building a cathedral?

Action Ideas:

1. Get down to the basic "Whys" in your business. NY Times Best-selling author, Simon Sinek said it best, "People don't buy what you do, they buy why you do what you do."

2. Share examples of how your products/services make a difference for the greater good. For example, instead of the airline, Jet Blue, focusing on simply "flying passengers safely to their destinations," their mission is to "... to inspire humanity – both in the air and on the ground." Now THAT'S a calling!

3. Ask your employees **why** they do what they do for your company. Pay attention to their answers.

Give your branded merchandise to your team.

Your customers may or may not appreciate your logoed apparel – but your employees will. Think about creating a "Welcome Basket" for your new hires. Share your company merchandise with the people who are proudest to wear it.

Do not make your employees pay for the products. Either give it to them for free or provide them with an allowance to choose what they would like to have. If they want to pick something out for a family member, let them.

Wearing company branded merchandise outside the workplace is a great conversation starter. When people see your branded apparel, they may ask your employees about your company. You may uncover a referral source for recruiting new hires.

My husband's company takes this concept to heart. Each year every team member receives a specially branded t-shirt. It's always fun to see the annual design, and he now has quite the collection. A fun t-shirt is an inexpensive way to engage.

Action ideas:

1. Allow team members to design a t-shirt, coffee mug, or other specialty item for the company to use. Encourage them to let their creative juices flow and create a unique giveaway.

2. Do not consider work-oriented items as "gifts." Giving inexpensive stationery or cheap ballpoint pens that employees have daily access to using can be construed as meaningless.

3. Choose gifts that are gender-neutral and that the staff will like and be proud to use or wear. Not sure? Ask for ideas.

Express your gratitude.

Do you want your employees to give you their very best efforts? Thank them when they do an excellent job. Look to catch them doing things well and acknowledge them for their hard work.

If you're thinking, "Why should I thank my staff? Isn't that what a paycheck is for?" you're missing the point. Employees who don't feel appreciated will work just hard enough not to get fired, because they're probably earning just enough so they don't quit.

Pay attention to those "Steady Eddies" – the people that are neither rock stars nor "problem children." They show up, do the work, and go home. You may be the first person in "Eddie's" career to notice the excellent job he/she is doing. Once noticed, that employee may put forward more effort and you'll see a positive change in their level of commitment.

In her TED talk, Dr. Laura Trice shares that being appreciated is one of those things that motivates us, both at work and in life. She notes the importance of making it clear when we want to be appreciated. If you feel underappreciated in your relationships, make it clear to the people in your life how you feel. The people who care about you will be more than willing to make sure they let you know how much they care about you.

"Thank you" ideas:

1. Handwrite a personalized thank you note

2. Put a letter of appreciation in the employee file

3. Send handwritten cards to mark celebratory occasions

4. Create an employee bulletin board and post recognitions

5. Note staff contribution in the company newsletter

Ask for positive and not-so-positive workplace attributes.

When you hear positive comments from your staff, keep a list of everything mentioned. Over time, you will build a list of testimonials that you can share with potential hires.

You also want to regularly ask your staff what they would change if given a chance. In cases where you can modify and improve their circumstances, go ahead and do it. By asking the question, you may be surprised at how little it takes to make a difference in your employees' satisfaction level.

When your staff knows you are listening to them, they are more likely to be engaged, which increases your retention levels. By focusing on what is working and taking care of what is not, your employees will realize that they have it pretty good. They will be less likely to fall prey to "the grass is greener over there" syndrome, and leave you for a competitor.

With a shrinking pool of qualified talent available to hire, it's crucial that you find out early if problems are brewing. Don't wait until your employee wants to leave before you act.

Here are some specific questions to get started:

1. If you were in charge, what changes would you make?

2. What do you hear from your clients about our company?

3. What do you like best about working here?

4. What don't you enjoy doing? Why?

5. What other areas are you interested in pursuing?

6. How can I help you reach your goals / become more successful?

Schedule time for a meal with individual employees.

When you break bread with the people you work with, you learn a lot about each other, develop friendships, and have real conversations. Spending time with individuals (or small groups when necessary) can create a real connection between you and the members of your staff.

Sharing a meal with individuals is not always possible when you have lots of employees working in different departments. You may have a remote staff or flexible scheduling policies that make it difficult for you to get together with everyone. Do the best you can with what you have.

Getting out of the office gives you time to refresh. It sets the example that the lunch break is just that – a break from work. Ask the other person where THEY prefer to go for lunch – and go. Don't complain or make up excuses. Get out of your comfort zone and try something new. This is not about you!

Action ideas:

1. Make a goal to go out to eat with each of your direct reports at least once this year. Encourage all your managers to do the same. The extra time you spend getting to know your employees will be well worth the investment.

2. Put down your phone and focus on the person with whom you are sharing a meal. Better yet, turn your phone over on the table, or keep it in your purse or briefcase to minimize the distraction.

3. Stick to a reasonable budget for food, and let employees know the parameters. By doing this, you will establish a sense of fairness and equal treatment amongst team members.

Shape up or ship out your disrespectful managers.

High turnover in a department may be a sign that it's the manager who needs to go. Your leadership team should reflect the type of culture you want for your company. Do not tolerate bullies in your workplace. Because bullying is a hot topic, employees and employers are now taking a more pro-active stance to confront the problem.

Make it safe for your employees to share concerns about their manager. Incorporate 360-degree reviews and keep the feedback anonymous so that employees share what they think. Please do NOT analyze each response and handwriting samples to figure out who said what. Just pay attention to the feedback and ACT on the suggestions contributed.

You may not like every person that works for you, but you must show them respect. If you can't be nice, be neutral.

Action Ideas:

1. Offer leadership development programs to ensure your leaders know the proper care and handling of employees.

2. Model best practices. Look for managers who are doing well and use their strategies to benchmark the rest of the team.

3. Document, document, document! To remove a manager who is unable or unwilling to change their tactics, make sure you can show, in writing, that you have done everything possible to rehabilitate them. You may have to prove that you had no choice but to fire them. This proper documentation will save you from a wrongful termination lawsuit.

Celebrate special occasions.

A study of more than one million respondents that was published by the Harvard Business Review found that employees use anniversary dates as a time to switch jobs. There is a big spike at the one-year mark and then at each successive anniversary.

Pay attention to these dates by giving your employees VIP treatment for their milestone anniversaries. Hire a limo to pick them up, give them a shout out on social media or your website, or pay attention to the things they like, and plan their day accordingly. Keep in mind that some employees like public recognition more than others.

You can also recognize anniversaries by giving employees a menu of choices of how they would like to be honored. Options may include: lunch with a C-Suite Executive or with their manager; leaving an hour early, or having a longer lunch; getting a chair massage (from a paid masseur, of course), receiving a unique company logoed item. Be creative and put together a list that works for you and your budget.

What are some creative ways you can recognize your team members' significant milestones?

_____

_____

_____

_____

_____

_____

Small rewards = Big smiles.

A client wanted to do something special for her support staff for "National Administrative Assistant's Day." Although Patty was looking for a "one-size-fits-all" approach, she realized that she could serve her team better if she put together a gift bag containing the specific things that each member likes.

She started by sending out an interest survey and then took the time to personalize and assemble individualized gift bags. The staff members were thrilled with the special attention she spent on each gift. Patty didn't need to spend a lot of money to make an impact; it was the attention to detail that mattered.

When you treat your employees as individuals and pay attention to their likes and dislikes, they will return the favor by putting their best efforts forward.

Action Ideas:

1. Create a survey to discover your employees' favorite things. Include small, medium and large items – from candy to spare time activities and maybe even vacation spots.

2. During the year, pay close attention to the things that delight your employees. Look for incidents and events that make them smile and keep notes that you can refer to in the future.

3. If employees don't want to participate, do the best you can based on what you know about the person.

Reward employees for outstanding customer service.

The better you treat your employees, the better they will take care of your customers. When someone goes above and beyond, make sure you share how that employee made a difference to the customer and to your company.

When an employee receives a "kudos" letter from a customer, share their achievement with the team and with upper management. Let your staff know how these positive actions make a difference to the customer and to the company. You may want to hang the letters on a bulletin board so everyone can see exactly what the employee to serve the client.

One industry that actively seeks out direct feedback opportunities is the hospitality industry. Many hotels give out business cards with Trip Advisor information on them to make it easy for their customers to share their experiences with the world. What are some ways can adapt their process in your industry?

Action ideas:

1. Create a "kudos" wall. When you receive letters from customers, put them in a public place so the rest of your team can see them. Give a framed copy to the employee mentioned.

2. Share it up the line. Recognition from upper management motivates employees to take more opportunities to be outstanding.

3. Publicize customer service achievements by using pictures of deserving staff on the cover of your company newsletter. Mention employees throughout the contents of your newsletter as well.

Acknowledge your Veterans.

Because of the number of troops being withdrawn from overseas and the military's increasingly tighter budgets, U.S. businesses are primed to see an unprecedented number of service members transitioning from the military to civilian life.

What does this mean for you? With approximately 1.5 million service members coming back into workforce in the next three to five years, you'll have opportunities to add these veterans to your staff. Hire them and take advantage of the skills, discipline and loyalty that they bring with them to your company.

Because the military already puts immense importance on formal recognition, finding ways to acknowledge them can be relatively easy to do. Make a point to honor your vets for their service.

Here are a few ideas from the Michael C. Fina (MCFRecognition.com) website for honoring your veteran employees.

1. Hold a Pinning Ceremony: Gather your vets together and present them with pins that represent their branch of service.

2. Give a "Salute Package": Make Veteran's Day special by giving them a small gift, a handwritten note, and a formal certificate.

3. Increase Veteran Awareness: Ensure that your employees are aware of the veterans working for you, so they can thank your veterans for their service in their own unique way.

Host an employee appreciation picnic.

Whether it's hot dogs and potato salad in the parking lot for employees only, or a full-blown offsite company picnic with families in tow, look for ways to build friendships while having fun in a casual atmosphere.

My husband's company holds their annual picnic at a large amusement park. Each employee gets two free tickets and a discounted rate for their family members. Most employees attend the event because they not only enjoy the fellowship, they like to see each other's kids as they grow up. There are employees who have worked there ten, twenty, thirty years and more – so there is a lot of history to share between the families.

The company holds a huge raffle at the park where the executives reward the winners with everything from grills to large screen TVs. The interesting thing about the lottery is that management cannot win. The primary goal is to thank and honor the hourly employees who work in the plant.

These employees work hard all year, and this picnic is just one of the many ways that management thanks them for their contributions.

What are some ideas that you can use to host an employee appreciation event?

_____

_____

_____

_____

_____

Send birthday cards with gift cards enclosed.

Give your employees small tokens of your appreciation on their special day. How do you know which gift card to include? Ask!

Find out your employees' favorite coffee shops, restaurants, or other services that have a gift card associated with them. Your employees may not remember telling you their choice or filling out a form, but when they open the card, they will notice that you care enough to pay attention to what they like.

Most grocery stores and other retail outlets offer a wide variety of gift cards. It's no longer necessary to go to one store and buy a stack of cards to dole out. Make it personal.

Have the card signed by management with a handwritten note, thanking them individually for what they do to make a difference in the company. The more specific, the better.

You don't have to spend a lot of money to make someone's day. It really is the thought that counts.

Action Ideas:

1. Shake it up! Every year, give your employee a different gift from their list. Doing the same thing repeatedly creates an expectation – Boring! Make it a surprise.

2. Choose or create personalized cards that mean something to their recipient. Cat person? Dog person? Baseball fan? Choose that card.

3. Give your managers a "birthday budget" to work with – and make sure they use it in full. Because all employees are included, you create a sense of fairness throughout the company.

Let your leaders serve your team.

Yes, cash is one of the ways you can reward your employees. Unfortunately, the cash "high" is short-lived. Money is not a long-term motivator. However, using money in conjunction with other incentives can be a great enticement. By creating experiences, you'll find plenty of ways to spur your team to higher levels of engagement.

Because monetary rewards are generally used to pay bills or take care of everyday expenses, employees often don't remember what they did with the cash received. You want to connect with staff in a more personal way. In doing so, you'll increase your team's loyalty, work ethic, and productivity.

Why not have a contest where the prizes include being served by the company leaders? Maybe your managers can serve lunch, wash employees' cars, or make a gourmet coffee run. Let your imagination run wild.

Action Ideas:

1. Provide a catered meal and have your leadership team serve your employees. Make sure managers are good sports about it and that they dish up the food with a smile.

2. Have a contest where the prize is having the employee's car washed or detailed by their manager in the parking lot.

3. Set up a dunking machine or a pie-throwing contest in your company parking lot and let your employees have at it. These are some of the ways to show that you're willing to have some fun at your expense for the good of the team.

Make recognition tangible.

Reinforcing good behavior must consistently happen if it is to be meaningful. By using tangible recognition practices every day at all levels of the organization, you'll reinforce the positive actions of your workers and create a culture of appreciation.

If you spot an employee cleaning up a mess that someone else made, why not hand him/her a "Kudos Card" for their part in making the workplace a bit nicer/safer? No, you don't have to hand out a reward every single time you notice an employee doing something kind for another. However, it doesn't take long for staff to notice that their managers are paying attention to the good that they do.

Designing and printing a reward card is a wonderful way to supplement a more formal recognition program. Create additional cards for employees to recognize their peers. Then, each quarter, have a raffle with prizes drawn from the cards received. Be creative and maximize the fun.

Some ideas for tangible recognition include:

1. Print "thumbs up" sticky notes and give them to managers and employees to recognize each other in the moment. Be sure to write on the note exactly what the employee did to deserve the appreciation.

2. Buy some decent sized rocks and, when a situation warrants acknowledgement, have employees sign this "You Rock" award.

3. Have a supply of thank you notes or postcards on hand for employees and managers to write to each other. Challenge people to write a certain number each month.

Write it down.

When you tell someone you appreciate them, you create a great memory; when you write it down, you create a treasure. Give your team concrete evidence of a job well done.

Whether you scribble "You're awesome!" on a Post-It note, write a thank you note, or compose a letter of appreciation, make sure to put your thoughts in writing. If you're wondering the difference between the last two – (in the author's opinion) a thank you note is for something specific while a letter of appreciation expresses the positive traits the employee has.

You can also give these appreciation letters to employees who went through a tough time and came out shining. Take the time to notice their successful comeback. By giving this type of approbation to employees after they face a difficult period in their lives, you'll show how much you value them.

Action Ideas:

1. Purchase a photo frame with a voice recorder in it. Place a certificate of appreciation inside, and include a personally recorded message of appreciation.

2. Record a brief video on your phone, embed it in an email or use a webinar service to thank your employee "in person." Make it short, personal, and unexpected. You'll make their day.

3. When you write a handwritten note to a team member, include a copy in their personnel file.

Train managers to use "on the spot" recognition.

Managers generally treat their employees the same way they were treated by their managers before them. Providing recognition is not an inherent skill, so make sure that ALL your managers are giving positive feedback to their staff. Train your managers in the art of effectively thanking employees for a job well done. Having a physical item to hand to an employee in the moment makes the gesture more meaningful.

Employees at all levels should feel that their contributions matter to the success of the organization – because they do. Blue collar, white collar, plant employees and administrative professionals alike should be acknowledged for their efforts.

If you wait too long to acknowledge the good that an employee does, they may not associate the action with the reward, thus reducing the impact. Remember, what gets recognized, gets repeated, so acknowledge positive actions.

Action Ideas:

1. If your managers are uncomfortable praising their employees, educate them on the ultimate value to the bottom line and to the company culture. Offer training to help them understand the value of their acknowledgement.

2. Make sure the award is perceived as meaningful and valuable. Don't make it about the money; recognize the specifics of job well done.

3. Require your managers to acknowledge a minimum number of employees each month. It will make them realize they must concentrate on employee strengths instead of always trying to fix what's broken.

PART 2

From this day forward

"I think as a company, if you can get those two things right — having a clear direction on what you are trying to do and bringing in great people who can execute on the stuff — then you can do pretty well." – Mark Zuckerberg, CEO, Facebook

Have fewer meetings.

Face it, unless there's food, no one enjoys going to the time-suck event known as a meeting. Yes, it is important for everyone to find out what's going on. However, most of the time, sharing short, specific updates is just as effective.

When you do need to meet, have an agenda that includes a hard start, and a hard stop. Ask for input and stick to the schedule. Respect your employees' time by giving them the opportunity to plan their day more efficiently.

Even though you might like to, you are not going to eliminate all meetings. Often, you can reformat your sessions to avoid the time-wasting aspects and get a lot more done. Your team members should feel energized rather than exhausted at the end of your time together.

Action Ideas:

1. Have a hard start and hard stop. If it's not on the agenda, you don't have to talk about it. Invite only those people who need to be present, and allow them to leave when they complete their part of the discussion.

2. Generate a realistic action plan for ideas/projects discussed. Hold people accountable for completing their assigned tasks.

3. Regularly meet with team members one-on-one for status updates and to connect with them personally. You can get together more frequently if you keep the sessions "short, sweet, and to the point" – five to fifteen minutes is ideal.

Make up your own holiday.

Break up the monotony of traditional office attire by having a theme day where you encourage employees to dress up for the occasion. Whether you choose Halloween, the eighties, or the first day of Spring, let your employees have some fun. Setting up a photo booth for group pictures is a terrific way to capture the moment.

Hold a desk or department decorating contest and give the winners a small prize. You can choose a theme or let each group pick their own. You'll create a sense of camaraderie and can use this as a team building activity.

Keep it simple. You don't have to spend a lot of money to do this. Encourage creativity by challenging your team members to spend as little money as possible.

To make sure employees are comfortable, no matter their belief system, you may want to stay away from traditional holidays. Use Chase's Calendar of Events, at chasescalendarofevents.com, for unique celebration ideas – or just make up your own holiday.

Unique celebrations ideas:

_____

_____

_____

_____

_____

_____

Offer flex time where possible.

Enable employees to determine how, where, and when they work. Focus on successful outcomes instead of the details of how the employees perform their jobs. Hold your team members accountable for their performance and give them the flexibility they want and deserve.

Yes, it's difficult to give up control, but what if there is a better way? Are you so focused on getting the job done your way, that you close yourself off to opportunities?

Cutting down on their commute shows that you care about giving your team members their time back. Yes, occasionally there will be employees who you need to monitor to make sure they are not abusing the extra flexibility, but it is often better to err on the side of trust.

Action Ideas:

1. **Do your homework.** Not all positions are conducive to non-traditional work hours. The work still needs to get done. However, there are probably more opportunities for flexibility than you think.

2. **Put it in writing.** Make sure your policy is detailed, clear, and nondiscriminatory. Consider positions, not people when creating your plan.

3. **Consider incorporating core hours.** For example, you may require everyone to be in the office from 9:00 – 3:00. However, employees can choose to work from 7:00 – 3:00, 9:00 – 5:00 or a different combination that works best for them.

Start your meetings on a positive note.

Instead of jumping right into business, begin each meeting by letting employees share a bit of good news. The stories shared can be personal or business related. Keep the updates short, so you have time to take care of business. By starting meetings in this manner, you'll shift the energy and launch the rest of the agenda on a more forward-thinking note.

Here are a few ideas that work:

1. Start each meeting by letting participants share "Thirty Seconds of Good News." Have a timer to keep the stories quick and maximize the number of people who can share.

2. Come up a simple challenge to kick off your meeting. This could be a current business challenge or a riddle. Even a simple challenge will get people thinking creatively and you'll have a productive meeting from start to finish.

3. Take an cue from Rotary Clubs who have a "Happy Bucks" segment. Members pay a dollar to share good news. The money collected goes to a charity the club supports, and everyone at the meeting gets to share in the celebration.

How can you create moments to share good news?

_____

_____

_____

_____

_____

_____

Offer a healthy meal.

According to Emil Shour from SnackNation, "More and more companies have realized that providing snacks in the office isn't just a 'nice to have.' It's practically required if you want to retain top talent."

Take steps to help your employees remain happy and healthy by educating them on proper nutrition and giving them access to information and trying new things.

There's a quote that says that we spend the first half of our life using our health to get wealth and the second half of our life using our wealth to get our health back. Let's start early and provide the means for a healthy team.

Here are a few ways to offer healthy meal choices:

1. **Set up a smoothie station.** Have a variety of fruits, nuts, protein powders, vegetables, etc., and let employees choose from a menu or create their own concoction. (Make sure you have one person running the machine – for convenience and safety's sake.)

2. **Bring in varieties of unusual fruits** so your employees can learn about them and try something they might not buy on their own. Check out the many companies that deliver fresh fruit directly to you every week.

3. **Encourage your vegetarian and vegan employees** to whip up a few of their favorite creations to demonstrate alternatives to having meat with every meal.

Expand your bereavement policy.

As the population ages, you may find more of your employees dealing with the death of a loved one. Although most policies give workers three days for immediate family, primary caregivers may need at least a week to deal with all the logistics surrounding death and burial.

If the relative lives out of state, it creates a more significant burden on the employee who has limited time off. Also, employees need time to process their loss, grieve their loved one, and figure out their new normal.

If they come back too soon, they are probably not going to be very productive. It's impossible to park your grief at the door and then pick it up at five. Show compassion and give your employees the time they need to heal.

Take a page from Facebook. Their generous bereavement policy gives employees 20 days' paid leave to mourn the death of an immediate family member and 10 days for an extended family member.

Don't make your employees choose their job over their family – nothing good comes out of that.

Ideas for expanding the current leave policy:

_____

_____

_____

_____

_____

_____

Acknowledge losses appropriately.

Suffering a significant loss is difficult. Going through a tough time without the support of your coworkers can make a difficult situation even harder to bear. Because people often don't know what to say to an employee who is going through a tough time, they usually say nothing at all.

Whether a team member loses a family member, a close friend, or a pet, acknowledge the loss in a heartfelt manner. Even though you may find it difficult to find the right words to say, just say something.

Small gestures can have a significant impact. By expressing your concern, verbally or in writing, you show your staff that you care about them and their family. They feel supported by your team.

Action Ideas:

1. **Express your sympathy** in person, over the phone, or in a card. Contact the employee as soon as you hear of their loss to let them know they are in your thoughts.

2. **Offer to help** with the employee's tasks at work. Send food or look for other ways to provide support for them at home.

3. **Donate to a suitable charity** in their loved one's name.

4. **Check in** and make sure your employee is doing all right.

5. **Remember that grief comes and goes** as time passes. Be patient.

6. **Encourage your employee** to take advantage of your company's employee assistance program (EAP) if they need additional help and support.

Focus on your staff's safety, ergonomics, comfort.

Your physical workplace environment contributes to the organization and quality of your employees' work. Physical comfort during the workday impacts employee motivation, performance, satisfaction, and engagement.

No, you don't have to buy the $2500 ergonomic chair if the $250 model or a simple back support device will work. Investing in your employees' health and safety will also keep you out of court. Disgruntled employees like to call places like OSHA, and you don't want to be at the wrong end of their investigation.

The degree to which your team members can personalize their work environment or control aspects such as lighting, temperature, and sound can make a huge difference in their motivation level.

When your workforce sees that you are paying attention to their basic needs ahead of bottom-line profits, you'll see both productivity and profits increase.

Action Ideas:

1. Use natural elements. Include plants, trees, windows, wood, and stone in workplace design to stimulate creative thinking.

2. Choose your colors wisely. Research shows that cool colors including blue and green can stimulate performance levels.

3. Don't forget sounds and scents. Elements like classical music enhance focus. The smells of lemon, jasmine, cinnamon, and vanilla have also been found to spur creativity and innovation.

Keep your head count lean.

People would rather be busy than bored, so running lean will help you keep your team active and engaged throughout the workday. Time goes a lot more quickly when you're not watching the clock.

The great recession of 2007 – 2009 gave many companies the opportunity to run a very tight operation to stay in business. If you must make a choice, it's better to err on the side of too few employees than too many. You want to have all your shifts covered, and have adequate backup. You also don't want to overwork and burn out your staff.

Create cross-training programs to help employees develop skills across a broad area. Not only will you have a more skilled workforce, but you'll also be able to keep employees busy when there is less demand for their primary skills. During the process, you may learn that your staff has skills that you did not know they possessed.

Action Ideas:

1. If your job descriptions are not current, work with your employees to make the necessary changes so they reflect actual day-to-day responsibilities.

2. Update your job descriptions regularly. Not only will it keep you safe legally, but your employees will know what the company expects from them.

3. Ask for honest, open feedback on employee workloads. If your staff is getting burned out, bring in temporary help to alleviate the pressure of "too much to do and not enough time to do it."

Offer bonus time off.

Time is our most valuable commodity. Therefore, when work schedules allow, letting employees leave an hour or two early as a reward for completing a project is very much appreciated.

The smartphone has pretty much eliminated any semblance of work/life balance because we are now connected 24/7. Granting your staff the chance to recharge for a couple of hours and get some personal work done means a lot.

A great example from my hometown was the day of the victory parade celebrating the Cleveland Cavaliers basketball championship. More than 1.25 million people packed the streets of downtown Cleveland for this historic moment. Instead of forcing their staff to come in (considering no Cleveland sports team had won ANY championship since 1964) many companies closed for the day to let their employees attend the parade.

Instead of enduring a painfully non-productive work day, companies benefited from the energy and enthusiasm of rejuvenated employees returning to work the next morning.

For what types of occasions could you offer bonus time off?

_____

_____

_____

_____

_____

_____

Bring in a treat.

Look for ways to reward your staff with seasonal treats. Some ideas - in the summertime, hold an ice cream social; in the fall, bring in apple pie. Make it nice. Don't be a cheapskate – that can backfire.

Learn a lesson from a company that hired an ice cream truck to come to their facility and sell their employees ice cream cones for one dollar. Company leaders thought that by giving employees a break and a cheap snack, they would appreciate the effort. They didn't.

Employees didn't understand why they had to pay for the ice cream. (No good deed goes unpunished, right?) If management had considered the few hundred extra dollars as an investment in their employees and a reward for the excellent work they do, they probably would have seen a much more grateful reaction.

A few ideas to get you started:

1. Bring in a variety of food trucks and let employees choose what and where they want to eat. You may or may not want to subsidize the purchase. Make an event out of it.

2. Arrange for mid-week treats in the breakroom. Waffle Wednesdays? Tuesday afternoon cookie platter? Taco Thursdays? Make sure you do health food events too!

3. On a hot day, have your managers give out ice cream bars. On a cold day, make the rounds with hot chocolate.

The key is to change it up often and keep it interesting. If you bring in pizza or bagels every Friday, it won't take long for it to become an expectation and not a treat.

Share in your employees' love of their "furry children."

Organize a "cutest pet" photo contest and let your employees vote for the winners. Give pet toys or treats for prizes. For those workers who don't have pets, let them find creative ways to participate if they'd like to.

Pet photos do not have to be limited to the animals that employees currently own. Maybe it's a favorite photo of a beloved pet that is no longer with them. Perhaps there's a friend or family member's pet they can include. Get creative and have a story that goes along with it, so employees can learn more about the "pet personality" that makes that pet worthy of the recognition.

Have different cat-agonies (pug, I mean pun intended) such as cutest pet, silliest pet, animals in action, best costume, etc. Get creative! Show your employees that you care about their furry family members too!

Pet-friendly Ideas and Examples:

1. Genentech provides discounts for dog daycare, or pet insurance that covers all sorts of pets

2. Salesforce allows employees to book a special room so their employees' dogs can have a comfortable day at the office. Amenities provided include soundproofed walls, water bowls, padded cages, dog beds, and cleaning wipes.

3. Build-a-Bear Workshop has parties to celebrate dog birthdays, treats, and even a canine concierge service that whisks the dogs off to a spa day with grooming and day camp.

Create a more positive workplace.

The book, "Strengths Finder" by Tom Rath shows readers why it's essential to develop their strengths instead of focusing on their weaknesses. When you focus the good things about your culture, you will create a more engaged workforce.

Look for ways to inspire your employees with positive quotes, success posters, and affirmations. Post them in high traffic areas, share them in your company newsletter, and ask your employees to share their personal favorites.

Model the behavior you'd like your employees to replicate. How can you "pay it forward" and encourage people to perform random acts of kindness throughout the day?

Action ideas:

1. Place a notebook or ledger by the office entrance. When employees arrive, invite them to share a happy thought, a quote, or something they were grateful for before starting their workday.

2. Put up a Gratitude Wall." Encourage employees to write positive notes, share good news or simply draw a smiley face. Make it colorful and fun. When the board gets filled, take a picture, wipe it down and start over.

3. Have a supply of thank you notes available for staff to access and use for their clients and for each other. Set aside some time each week, like Jimmy Fallon does on The Tonight Show, to allow employees to write and deliver these notes. Keep track of how many notes are sent each week and celebrate your total count of people thanked at the end of the year.

Hire a photographer to take
professional headshots.

Portray your employees in their best light by taking individual and departmental photographs. Great photos elicit an emotional response, and people want to feel good about themselves. Give them the opportunity to do so.

By providing pictures for your employees' use, you help them look more polished in their social media and other profiles, thereby representing your company more professionally. The grainy images employees cut and post from vacation photographs do not help them look very well-qualified.

Incorporate your staff's current, relevant photos into personalized greeting cards as a terrific way to connect with your customers. Take fun group shots and include them on thank you notes and holiday cards. Have team members personally sign the cards.

Use these photos to put together an org chart with everyone's picture on it. You will give new employees the opportunity to learn who's who in the organization – not only by their title but by their face.

Creative ways to use company photos include:

_____

_____

_____

_____

_____

_____

Take pictures and put them on display.

These days, practically everyone has a high-quality camera that they carry around with them at all times – their phone. Use that tool to have a little fun in the workplace.

Take pictures of your team, print them out, and hang them on a wall or keep them around the office. Capture a variety of moments – department pictures, event photos, random shots, even what my siblings like to call "stupid family photos." Have fun with it.

Why not have company photo contests and see how many fun, impromptu, action shots you can collect. Have a caption contest for some of the hilarious pictures – and keep it family-friendly, of course.

Sharing photos might not seem like a big deal, but it's a gesture that helps your employees feel like they are part of the team.

Where can you share?

1. Social media – let potential employees know what a great place your company is to work. Stop being so boring on Facebook!

2. Bulletin boards – change them up every so often, so people get in the habit of looking to see what's new.

3. Photo slideshows – Loop on TVs in the lobby or break room. Show the photographs during company events. People will watch because they want to see themselves. It's always good for a smile.

Let the music play!

The power of music to enrich our lives has been known pretty much since the beginning of time. When you allow your employees to listen to music at work, you can bring that benefit into the workplace as well.

Researchers from Cornell University discovered that when employees hear happy, upbeat music, they tend to be more productive, cooperative, and they work harder. Studies show a 14 percent increase in productivity for workers who perform simple tasks while listening to music and a 6.3 percent increase in productivity for workers doing other types of work. Listening to music helps employees do monotonous jobs more efficiently, which may give your business an economic boost.

Really, why would you NOT allow your employees to get a little "musical motivation" during the day?

Action Ideas:

1. Let your employees wear earbuds while performing work they can do by themselves.

2. Make sure that safety concerns are taken care of: for example, you might require that employees conceal any wires from earbuds under their clothing, so the cords don't get caught on anything.

3. For a company's intercom system, let team members be the "DJ for the day" and share their personal taste in music (Family friendly, of course)

Keep up-to-date with an intra-company newsletter.

Make your newsletter a fun source of information in the company. Interview employees from various parts of the business. Include fun facts and personal information (as much as they are willing to share).

As your employees discover they have common interests, you'll further encourage friendships to develop. As employees start to "cross the aisle" and get to know team members in other departments, you'll also improve communication levels.

In sharing success stories, make sure you include everyone. You'll not only give the featured employees the recognition and positive reinforcement they deserve, but you'll also give your team a reason to connect with each other.

Ideas for Newsletter features:

1. Success stories or customer spotlights

2. Industry news

3. Human interest stories

4. Educational articles

5. Coupons or special offers

6. Company Q&A

7. Employee surveys and results

8. Interviews

9. Product reviews

10. Let your imagination run wild!

PART 3

For Better or Worse

"We believe that it's really important to come up with core values that you can commit to. And by commit, we mean that you're willing to hire and fire based on them. If you're willing to do that, then you're well on your way to building a company culture that is in line with the brand you want to build." –
Tony Hsieh, CEO, Zappos

Have an "open-mind" versus an "open door" policy.

An actual "open door" policy is difficult to maintain. With heavy workloads and tight deadlines, you just don't have the time for employees to pop in and ask you a question. After all, if they know they can always come to you to solve their problems, what incentive do they have to figure it out on their own?

An open mindset in company leadership is a vital, enduring, and rewarding part of having an engaged culture. This authentic approach plays a critical role in inspiring your employees to operate with an open mind as well.

An "open mind" policy shows that you are open to frank discussion and you will set appropriate boundaries that work for you and your team, and still lets the work get done. Let your employees know that you are there for them when they truly need you, but empower them to solve some of their nagging issues on their own.

Action Ideas:

1. Make sure that no matter what you hear, you don't "kill the messenger." Listen without interruption and ask for your employee's suggestion in solving the issue.

2. Have a "thanks for sharing" attitude instead of a "yeah but" attitude. If you fight or argue about the points that your team member is trying to make, they will stop sharing.

3. Never ask a question that you don't really want the answer to. Become a master of the "Poker Face" and provide a haven for employees to share their thoughts and ideas with you.

Learn from and benchmark top performers.

When you notice your "rock star" employees accomplishing remarkable things, take the time to acknowledge what they are doing differently than everyone else. Incorporate their ideas and methods into new hire training. Utilize these best practices to benchmark what other departments are doing. Always look for ways to improve your processes.

If one employee figures out a tactic that works, don't let his/her efforts go to waste. When a person is doing something well, there's a good chance that others can use those same ideas in their jobs as well.

Regularly interview your top talent from time to time and "go to school" on the answers they give you. When your team members see that you're acting on their suggestions and giving them credit for the ideas, they are more likely to keep sharing.

Questions to ask:

1. What motivates you about your job?

2. What challenges you?

3. How/what do you delegate to others?

4. How do you communicate with your team?

5. What shortcuts have you discovered?

6. What resources do you still need?

7. How can we help?

Be enthusiastic about the future.

Unless you are confident in your company's capacity for success, how do you expect your employees to believe they have a stable future with you?

Be a cheerleader - no, not the kind with pom-poms. Encourage and support your team. Cheer them on. Broadcast the good things that are happening. Celebrate small victories. Create a culture where employees want to share their positive experiences, instead of just complaining about the tough times. When you incorporate optimistic news into your communications, you improve staff commitment, engagement, and understanding.

Bonus: It's easier to create content for your newsletter, blog, or marketing articles as you learn all the new and exciting stories you have to tell.

Action Ideas:

1. Keep an eye out for situations where your employees are making a difference and share it with the rest of your team.

2. Use good news as a learning opportunity. Share what happened and then cite the takeaways that can inspire others to model the positive behavior.

3. Make sure to help people get noticed when they participate. Provide multiple ways colleagues can respond and add to the good news, comment on the success of others, and share their own experiences in similar situations.

Flatten your organizational structure.

A flat company structure empowers your employees to take charge of their jobs, make better decisions and feel a higher level of responsibility for the company's success. By getting rid of some of the layers of management, you facilitate more communication as well. Asking your staff for their input leads to more support for the decisions made, and you won't see as many power struggles behind the scenes.

With a flatter organization, you'll reduce overall costs. Fewer levels of leadership mean you won't need as many employees, which means lower expenses for both payroll and office space. When you run with a lean staff, each person will have greater responsibilities to get their tasks done. You'll encourage more cohesion, better productivity and you'll get more work done.

Action ideas:

1. Don't make employees jump through a lot of hoops to share their thoughts. The only thing red tape halts is progress.

2. Give your staff access to leadership. It helps them feel like they are heard and can make a difference.

3. Realize that as the number of Millennial and Gen Z employees increase, you will see a shift away from the autocratic way of running a business. Listen as employees contribute their skills, knowledge, and education. Your best ideas may come from the least expected sources.

Be open and honest in sharing information.

A company went through a major restructuring. Instead of keeping their employees in the loop, management announced the changes over the course of two conference calls. During the first call, twelve people found out their jobs were "eliminated, effective immediately." During the second call, the HR Manager read the names of their colleagues caught up in the downsizing to the remaining staff.

Because everyone was caught unaware, it took the staff a long time to rebuild trust with leadership. Employees met every conference call with suspicion. They attended every meeting with a sense of fear. It took a long time for employees to have faith in management again.

If the organization had been up front and let their employees know that some changes may be coming, they could have minimized the long-term damage.

Action ideas:

1. Employees may not always like what you must tell them. Be upfront and tell them anyway.

2. When you restructure your organization for financial reasons, ask your employees for ideas on how to make a smoother transition. You may be surprised with their creativity and insight.

3. Make sure any employees you release due to cutbacks are thanked for their service and taken care of financially as much as you can.

Offer competitive wages and benefits.

Although managers may feel that they need to throw money at their employees to keep them engaged, this is not necessarily the case. However, if your current wage scale is not up to industry standards, you risk your employees leaving to go elsewhere for more money.

When employees are satisfied with their pay and benefits, they spend more time working and less time looking for better paying opportunities. When employees realize that their pay is fair when compared to other companies, it makes it easier for them to focus on the job at hand.

It is worth paying for high-quality talent. When everything else is equal, people take the higher paying job. When you get the right people onboard, you can save your company significant money in the long run in these three areas:

Healthcare. When your employees are engaged, they are likely to be healthier and less stressed. When you have healthy employees, you may be able to reduce the healthcare premiums you are paying.

Recruitment and training. If your employees are satisfied with their benefits, they are less likely to leave. With a more tenured team, you won't have to spend the time and money training new staff continually.

Productivity. Gallup research shows that workers who are "highly satisfied" with their jobs are up to 50% more productive at work.

Encourage management to mingle with the staff.

An HR manager shared that she requires her managers to learn the names of all the people that report to them. If supervisors are unwilling to make an effort to do this, she fires them. At first blush, that sounds a little extreme, doesn't it? Think about it - how would you feel about working for a boss that didn't even know your name? Yes, employees don't like it either.

Walk around your facility on a consistent basis and greet people by name. Look for reasons to have a short conversation when possible. Challenge yourself to find shared interests with your staff. It's true, some of your employees will be more willing to share their personal lives than others. Whichever way they respond is fine – it's making the effort that counts.

Action Ideas:

1. Regularly schedule time with each of your employees. Often, a simple five-minute check-in will suffice. Find out what's going on with team members personally and professionally.

2. Use icebreakers and other social activities that allow team members to learn interesting facts about each other and get to connect on a personal level.

3. If you're "not good" at remembering names, take steps to fix that. Dale Carnegie Training and other companies offer excellent guidance on recalling names.

Create strong relationships with your employees.

Your employees want you to see them as more than an employee ID number. They want to be "seen." You can build lasting relationships by starting simply. Find out what team members like and like to do. Are they cat people? Dog people? What are their favorite sports teams? Hobbies? Learn what they value, and they will appreciate your effort.

One icebreaker you can use is "Two Truths and a Lie." Here's how it works: Break into groups of up to eight people. Have everyone write down three statements, two of which are true, and one is a lie. Each person takes a turn reading their comments. The others in the group try to guess which one is the lie. The reader does not fess up until everyone has guessed. Keep track of how many people each person fools.

While using this activity during a workshop with a restaurant chain, we discovered that two of their kitchen managers had cooked for two different Presidents of the United States. Even the company owners did not know this. How cool is that?

Action Ideas:

1. Use short icebreakers to add spice to your meetings.

2. Organize activities that allow employees to spend time together as a group outside of the office.

3. Recognize your employees' achievements as they happen. Don't wait to acknowledge good work.

Get rid of toxic employees.

If you have employees working for you who have terrible attitudes, correct the situation or let those people go. A hostile "lone wolf" can do more damage than their productivity (or lack thereof) is worth to the rest of the team.

Of course, from a legal standpoint, documentation is critical. The goal of a progressive discipline process is retention, so do your best to get the problem employee back on track. Record what the employee did and the negative impact he/she had on the team. This action not only protects you from wrongful termination lawsuits, but it also shows that you made every effort to help the employee, but he/she chose not to do so.

Just one problem employee can destroy the culture of an organization. And, when a problem employee causes others to leave, who jumps ship - your worst employees or your best ones? Take the steps you need to create order and harmony amongst the staff.

Action plan:

1. Have a correction action plan in place. Offering coaching and retraining before the formal discipline process shows the effort you put forth to help your employee change.

2. Train your managers in proper documentation techniques. If it is not written down, it didn't happen.

3. There are no employees that you can't live without. It's never easy to fire someone, but sometimes that is your only option. It's a business decision. When the toxic person is gone, the rest of your team will breathe a sigh of welcome relief.

Allow open and honest feedback.

Some employees may be uncomfortable speaking their minds. There may be numerous reasons for this, but it's critical for you to create the space for them to do so. Promote and practice respectful candor. When employees don't feel they have a voice, they may hold back valuable information, ideas, and solutions that could propel your company forward. Don't be an "Emperor who is not wearing clothes" type of manager.

Notice that the optimal word here is "respectful." Play nice. Allowing honest communication goes not give people the license to be rude, crude, or mean-spirited.

If asking staff for feedback is new for you, start small. Acknowledge the responses you receive and encourage more detailed replies to your inquiries.

Action Ideas:

1. **Focus on your future.** Ask employees what management can do better going forward instead of focusing on what you did poorly in the past.

2. **Be specific about what you want.** Instead of the overly broad, "What do you think?" ask about particular parts of the project that you are discussing.

3. **Let employees vent without interruption.** Sometimes people need to let off steam and don't need you to "fix" anything. So long as venting doesn't become a habit, be okay with an occasional outburst.

Consistently conduct exit interviews.

It's often difficult when a valued employee decides to move on. Don't take any person's leaving your organization for granted. Every employee has a reason that they've decided to quit, and it's your job to find out why by consistently conducting exit interviews. Treat any information received as valuable data that will help you make needed improvements going forward.

The point of doing exit interviews is to use the information acquired. Some of it will be difficult to hear. There will be other things that you have no control over. Do what you can to make small changes and over time, you will see big results.

Here are a few of the topics you'll want to cover:

1. Overall job satisfaction/dissatisfaction

2. Specific reason for leaving

3. Frustrations experienced on the job

4. Their thoughts about the corporate culture

5. Relationships with supervisors and team members

6. Adequacy of compensation and benefits

7. Anything else you would like to know for future posterity.

By being consistent in your asking, over time, you'll see patterns emerge that are causing valued team members to take their skills away from your company. Act on our newfound knowledge and increase your retention rates.

Treat your staff better than you treat your customers.

Remember, your employees are your internal CUSTOMERS. How you take care of them is a good indication as to how they will treat your clients.

Are your priorities in this order? Employees first, Customers second, and Leadership third. If so, nice work! This is the correct order. Put the needs of your staff first. Take care of your team and treat them fairly. Exceed their expectations. When you set high standards for workers and empower them to do the right thing, they will treat your customers with the same regard.

As tough as it may be to hear, leadership ranks third on the list. The better you make your employees look, the more effort they will put forth for you. Also, remember to share the credit and accept the blame. Nothing is worse than a manager who throws their employees under the bus. Remember, if your employees are not performing at their best, the problem may be their boss.

Action Ideas:

1. Want to know what would make your employees happy? Ask them. The chances are good that they want/need much less than you expect.

2. Make sure you maintain your employee gathering areas as well you take care of management and client areas. A fresh coat of paint in the break room can make a huge difference in morale.

3. Tell your team how much you appreciate their contributions to the company. Make sure to acknowledge them verbally and in writing. And do it early and often.

Share successes up the organization.

Make sure that upper-level management is aware of significant employee contributions. When workers receive an acknowledgment from leadership, they feel valued. They realize that their boss is paying attention to who they are and what they do, thereby increasing their commitment level to the organization.

The recognition needs to be timely to feel authentic. When Rita won a national sales contest, it took her manager three weeks to personally congratulate her. By then, it was too late. A short time later, she left the company.

According to a Harris Poll of 1000 workers, 63% of employees feel that they do not receive recognition for their achievements. Forty-seven percent say their managers take credit for their ideas and 36% say their managers don't know their names. How do you prevent your workers from joining these statistics? Read on.

Action Ideas:

1. Ensure the amount of recognition matches the effort and the results. Overpraising for average performance makes the attempt less meaningful.

2. Be specific. Let your team member know the details of what they did to deserve such praise.

3. Copy upper management on the congratulatory emails you send to staff. Encourage leaders to post a positive reply to the employees recognized.

Acknowledge tenure in smaller increments.

To keep employees longer, try rewarding shorter terms of tenure. Depending on your turnover rate, why not give recognition for one-year or three-years of service – instead of waiting for a five-year anniversary before you acknowledge them.

Organizations who give service awards generate employee morale. Make a big deal of the event. A service award handed out without some pomp and circumstances does not achieve the same effect as when you expend your congratulations publicly.

The acknowledgment doesn't have to be big. A signed card by the leadership team with a personal note may be a nice touch – particularly if you send it to team members at home.

Action Ideas:

1. Write it down. Have all your employees and managers sign an anniversary card and encourage them to write a personal note. Form letters do not have the same effect.

2. Give a gift. Present your staff member(s) with a unique token of your appreciation for his/her years of dedicated service.

3. Let them eat cake. Find out what kind of cake or special treat your employee enjoys most and bring that in for them. Make sure you personalize the cake with their name and years of service.

Watch your facial expressions.

Smile. Greet your employees with a friendly face. People can not only see a smile; they can "hear" one as well, so remember this while you're on the phone. (Also, as one of my clients shared, a customer on the phone can also "hear" an eye roll.)

Author, Tonya Reiman says, "Smiling demonstrates confidence, openness, warmth, and energy. It also sets off the mirror neurons in your listener instructing them to smile back, she says. Without the smile, an individual is often seen as grim or aloof."

Your employees react to the expression they see on your face. When you are concentrating on what they are saying, with your brows furrowed, they may think you are angry with them. Try to keep your expression as neutral as possible when you are listening to what staff has to say.

Action ideas:

1. Make a point to say, "Hello," using your employee's name. Smile or at least nod when you walk by them. Your staff will see you as more friendly and approachable.

2. Keep a mirror by your phone and make sure you are smiling when you are speaking on the phone. It literally changes your tone of voice.

3. Know that the corners of your mouth tend to turn down as you age. Focus on keeping your lips slightly upturned, creating a warm expression.

Give tangible evidence of a job well done.

Express your appreciation verbally and/or write it on a note—even a post-it note will work. The recipient will NOT throw that piece of paper away!

Remember, when you tell someone you appreciate them, you create a memory. When you write it down, you create a treasure.

At a luncheon keynote, I shared the power of post-it notes. One attendee scribbled a plus sign on five sheets of paper and handed one to each person sitting at his table, letting them know how they were a positive influence in his life.

One of the receivers of the note excitedly shared with me how thrilled she was to receive this message. It meant a lot to her – and it was only a plus sign on a piece of paper. This stuff works!

Action Ideas:

1. Praise feels most sincere when you take the time to spell out details. Emphasize the actions that you'd like to see your staff do more often.

2. Demonstrate interest in your employees by regularly by asking about the events in their lives. Give small gifts that relate to what they share so employees know you're paying attention.

3. Have a supply of cards around and share them for no reason at all, to celebrate an employee's special day, or to offer sympathy when a colleague is ill or experiences a family death.

Give your undivided attention.

When your employee approaches you with a question, problem or issue, put down the phone, stop texting, look away from the computer. Make full eye contact, keep a neutral expression, and fully listen. Simply by being present, you are giving your employee a gift.

However, you don't always have time to give your employees the undivided attention they seek. Let him or her know that you are in the middle of something and schedule a time for you to have the conversation – and stick with it. Make your staff your priority, and you'll create a foundation of trust.

Keep yourself from distractions by muting your phone and turning it over on your desk, so you don't notice the texts, emails, and Facebook posts popping up.

Action Ideas:

1. Silence Your Devices. Turn off your alerts, notices, and anything else that can disrupt the flow of your conversation.

2. Don't Multi-task. Even if you are on the phone, people can tell when you're doing multiple things at once doesn't work. Stop and give your full attention to the person speaking to you.

3. Face the Person. When you look at someone face-to-face, it's a powerful way to demonstrate that they are holding your attention. You'll build both trust and stronger communication.

4. Listen first, then speak. Don't jump in and respond to everything an employee is sharing. Absorb and understand what they are saying and share your thoughts only when warranted.

Have your employees' backs.

When your staff knows that you will stand behind them, they are more likely to make better decisions, try new things, and take calculated risks than if they don't feel that you will support them. You foster a stronger sense of engagement when you build a foundation of trust with your team.

When mistakes occur, discuss what happened with your employee, and what they learned from the error. Then move on.

Your job as a leader is to share the credit during times of celebration and take the blame when things go wrong. When asked during informal polls during training sessions about their "worst manager of all time," the number one answer is the manager who throws them under the bus. Don't be that person!

Action Ideas:

1. Ask your subordinates how you can better support them. Be okay with whatever answer they give you and learn from the feedback.

2. Roll up your sleeves and pitch in to help when a staff member is in a pinch. No job should be below you – after all, you have team members that are performing those duties.

3. Be the first to acknowledge and celebrate the excellent work of your employees. As Dale Carnegie said, "Be lavish in your praise."

Schedule "stay" interviews

Just as you want to know why employees leave through exit interviews, it's also important to find out why they stay. Stay interviews help you retain current employees as you reinforce what is working for them and what changes can be made to keep them happy and productive in the job.

Focus on your employee's perspective on how things are going by taking a open approach in the conversation. Ask open-ended questions to find out about the employee's career goals, the aspects of their job that they like and any problem areas that may need to be addressed.

According to Human Resources Inc., here are some questions to include in your stay interviews:

- What are the things you like about your job?
- What keeps you motivated?
- What do you like best/least about the job?
- What would you like to learn this year?
- What would you like to change about your current job?
- What would make your job more enjoyable/rewarding?
- What would cause you to consider leaving the company?
- What is your ideal job, and how can we help your progress towards it?
- Do you feel encouraged in your career goals? How can we help you achieve your goals?
- Do you feel you receive recognition in your job?
- What kind of recognition would be most relevant?
- If you quit today, what would you miss most about the job? What would you miss the least?

Respond quickly.

Personally answer your phone when possible and respond to staff emails within 24 hours of receiving them. By taking the time to respond to your employees, you send a powerful signal that they are a priority. Your prompt action emphasizes their importance more than just your words ever could.

Because you have timelines, due dates, and priorities that need your attention, you do not always have the luxury of stopping what you are doing and addressing the employee's issue immediately. You can, however, explain the situation and schedule a more convenient time to connect with them. Then do it.

The extra time you spend paying attention to your workers will pay off in higher loyalty and commitment to your organization.

Action Ideas:

1. Respond immediately to an email or text to let your employee know you received their message.

2. For difficult conversations, do NOT respond via email or text. It's difficult to read emotion into a written document, and your employee may misinterpret what you are saying. Pick up the phone or meet them in person to convey difficult news.

3. Keep your employees in the loop. Let them know the status and any updates on their ideas and suggestions.

PART 4

For Richer or Poorer

"To build a culture of engagement it is important to incorporate training on intrinsic motivation and employee engagement into management development programs." ~ Kenneth Thomas

Continually refresh and enhance employee knowledge.

New employees automatically go through training. During this orientation period, they learn the company's mission, vision, rules, regulations and the conditions in which they will be working. Then they are taught how to perform their job.

Sometimes organizations tend to forget about their existing employees when it comes to refreshing and expanding their knowledge base. Make learning a constant in your company.

When you offer professional development opportunities to your team members, you'll help them to become better tomorrow than they are today, creating a highly skilled workforce in the process.

Ongoing training:

Improves employee morale. Training gives employees the feeling of job security and higher job satisfaction.

Requires less supervision. Well trained workers can get the job done with less time and effort.

Enhances promotability. As employees acquire advanced skills, they become a greater asset to the organization.

Reduces accident risk. Errors often occur because a lack of the knowledge and expertise required to do the job.

Increases productivity. Properly training employees require less time, money and resources to get the job done.

When you train, you will retain!

Make an investment in your team members.

During a conference presentation, I asked the audience members what they did to help their employees grow within the organization. One woman raised her hand and shared that her company gave each worker $1,500 per year to invest in whatever personal or professional studies they wanted.

You could hear the collective gasp, as one woman uttered out loud what everyone else was thinking, "We have 500 employees. We don't have that kind of money laying around." I asked the first woman, "How many of your staff take advantage of this offer?" She replied, "About 3-5% of them."

There's an old HR cartoon where the CFO and the HR manager are talking. The CFO asks, "Well, what if we invest all this money in training our employees and they leave?" To which the HR manager answers, "Yes, but what if we don't train them – and they stay?"

Think about it, would you rather have trained or untrained employees stay with your company?

Action Ideas:

1. Survey your employees to see what topics are of most the interest to them.

2. Make sure you present training opportunities as an investment in the employee, and not a punishment.

3. Offer "lunch and learn" sessions. It keeps the learning in-house, and those in attendance can carry on the conversation after the meeting is over.

Make your good leaders great.

Professional development training needs to be an ongoing part of your leadership's career path. No matter how long your managers have been with you, it's critical for your company's long-term success that you offer continuing education to keep their skills up to date.

By providing opportunities for growth, you create a trickle-down effect that benefits the entire organization. As your leaders learn the skills to manage their people better, they build a stronger, more cohesive team.

Training reinforces the good habits that leaders have and teaches them new ways of dealing with stressful situations. Choose a variety of programs that help leaders manage their time more efficiently, communicate more effectively, set realistic expectations, have difficult conversations and encourage feedback from managers, peers, and subordinates.

Conduct a portion of your programs in-house so that the participants can have the same conversation. Also, consider sending managers off-site to get a fresh perspective and interact with people from different industries.

Different types of training to consider offering to your leaders:

- Employee Relations
- Time Management and Planning
- Safety and Emergency
- Ethics and Harassment
- Human Resources
- Leadership and Supervisory
- Customer Service

Promote from within whenever possible.

When you promote from within, you substantially shorten the learning curve. Your employee already knows what the job entails. They understand the culture, and they are used to the company's procedures.

Look first to the people you already have on board, instead of risking hiring someone new who may or may not stick around. When staff members know they can move up within the company, they have a greater incentive to work hard and to stay with you.

Make sure you spend the time and money to train your new supervisors. When you take your best salesperson, and promote him/her based on their success in their current role, you may be creating your worst new manager without adequate training.

Action Ideas:

1. Look for potential lateral moves that give your employees the opportunity to use different skill sets. You may discover talents that you did not realize your team members have.

2. Give your employees a variety of continuing education opportunities from which they can choose. Then, keep an eye on those who take you up on your offer. These motivated team members may be your emerging leaders.

3. Empower your employees to do their job in the best way they see fit. Don't micromanage. Stay out of their way and make it safe for them to come to you if they have questions.

Develop training materials for specific situations.

Let your employees develop protocols based on real-life situations in the workplace. With a record number of baby boomers leaving the workforce, it's critical that you capture the knowledge and expertise that will soon be walking out the door. By planning ahead, you'll be better equipped to create procedures that endure for the future.

Be on the lookout for humorous or ridiculous customer service stories – share what happened, and the employee's favorable response to the situation.

If there wasn't a satisfactory conclusion, write down some of the lessons learned so that people know what NOT to do when that same situation occurs again.

How do you do this?

Assess Your Needs: What are the areas that your team needs the most assistance and support? Start there.

Design Your Materials: You may want to find articles you like and look for ways to adapt them to your specific needs.

Conduct Training Sessions: Make sure that all employees know and understand the material. Train groups of people so that they are on the same page.

Assess the Results: What went well? What would you change for next time?

Repeat.

Hold yourself and your managers to high standards.

Lead by example in all you do. Problems arise when managers do not follow the precedent they expect others to follow. Some of the reasons for poor performance may range from a lack of knowledge to overall sloppy practices. Correct whatever needs to be fixed and set the standard for excellence.

When leaders ignore unruly behavior because they don't want to deal with a problem employee or they overtly show favoritism to another staff member, it can be detrimental to employee morale. Your actions do speak louder than your words, so as Gandhi says, "Be the change you want to see."

Encourage 360-degree feedback and take heed of what employees share with you about their managers. Look for the golden nuggets in the responses you receive. Accept any criticism with "Thank you for sharing" and nothing more. If you argue, your staff will never give you their honest opinions again.

Action Ideas:

1. Set clear expectations about the outcome you want your leaders to achieve. Share how you'll measure their success

2. Consider each person's skills and capabilities to accomplish the task. Make sure they have the resources they need.

3. Agree on measurable, objective targets. Let your leaders know you'll be there for them when they need you.

4. Give honest, open, ongoing feedback on the manager's progress. It's more important to be helpful than nice.

"I love to be micromanaged," said no employee ever!

Don't be what Peggy Drexler of Forbes refers to as a "helicopter boss." When you hover over your employees, you create a barrier to trust. Yes, you want to check in with your staff regularly, but give them space. Show them that you trust them, and be there for them when they need your support.

Successful leaders look to the fact that the job is getting done correctly. As long as that's the case, they are not necessarily concerned with how it gets done. Give your employees the opportunity to do things the way they see fit. After all, if the employee completes the job on time and on budget, does it really matter if it's not done exactly the way you would have done it?

Action Steps:

1. If you tend to be a control freak, look for one "baby step" you can take to release control and let your employees succeed (or fail) on their own.

2. Think about your favorite boss of all time and write down the traits that you admire most about that person. What can you do today to model those traits for your team?

3. Give your staff plenty of opportunities to develop new skills. Note their strengths and let them further develop the skills they already have.

Treat employees fairly.

Treating your employees in a fair manner means that you take the time to get to know them and you understand their specific circumstances. If you have a staff member going through a tough time, it's likely that their performance may suffer. Let them know you have their back.

Remember, fair treatment does not necessarily mean equal treatment.

When employees see that you care enough to make exceptions when warranted, they will know you will also take care of them when they are facing a similar situation. However, when employees cross the line and take advantage of their situation, managers need to stop enabling problem behavior.

Because we are "wired" for justice, employees want to know they are getting a fair shake. Feelings of injustice lead to lost productivity, disgruntled workers and a lack of trust that results in high turnover and low morale.

Action steps:

1. Document both successes and transgressions to show that your decisions are fair-minded and just.

2. Ask your staff what they think are reasonable expectations for you to help them get back on their feet.

3. If your managers lack the skills necessary to appropriately manage, motivate, and discipline their workers, invest in leadership training.

Use mistakes as opportunities.

Create a safe environment for employees to admit when they've made an error.

There's a story from the early days of IBM of an engineer who made a mistake that cost the company a million dollars. The engineer came into Thomas Watson's office, knowing he was going to get fired. Instead, Mr. Watson asked him, "Why would I fire you? I just spent one million dollars educating you." He never made that blunder again.

In another situation, a Regional Manager made an error that almost cost the company their biggest client. After jumping through a lot of hoops, she saved the account. Now she begins her staff meetings with "Who messed up worse than I did this week, and what did you learn from it?" By being vulnerable with her own slip-up, this manager creates a safe environment for her staff to let her know the real story – instead of hiding the truth out of fear of reprisal.

In both cases, mistakes caused the employee, and the company, to grow in both knowledge and understanding.

Action Ideas:

1. Mistakes happen. If the lesson is learned, and the mistake is not repeated, move on. If you need to, watch the movie "Frozen" so you can learn to "let it go!"

2. See number one.

Create an onboarding process that rocks!

The chances are good that when your employee accepted your job offer, he or she was probably interviewing at other places too. Just because a person took your job doesn't mean that the calls with different offers will stop.

In their first two weeks of work, your employees are still deciding whether they want to stay or not. If they get an offer from another company that sounds better than what they have with you, you will lose them. All that time, money and effort you spent in hiring them will go for naught.

Some organizations have gone so far as to create viral videos that give prospects a feeling of what it's like to work there. Why not have some fun and show your candidates what a terrific organization they can join if they come on board with you.

Ideas for better onboarding:

1. Connect with new hires before they start

2. Make their first day memorable

3. Introduce them across department lines

4. Ease them into the paperwork

5. Set them up with a "lunch buddy"

6. Give them time to adjust to their new role

7. Communicate your culture to make sure they fit

Make sure that your new employee's first day is not leading up to their last day too quickly.

There's value in learning during lunch.

All work and no learning make for a dull team. Allow group leaders to hold "Lunch and Learn" sessions.

Set up a training portal that all your workers can access for their professional development – white collar, blue collar, hourly, and salary. There are many free and low-cost programs available online and offsite. Take advantage of them.

Giving your team opportunities to learn on their own helps you to figure out which staff members are self-motivated enough to embrace additional training (watch those people, they are your future leaders!).

When you offer "lunch and learns" events for anyone who wants to attend, you'll have a group of individuals in the same room, learning the same things, and having the same conversations. There is strength in numbers and the more the word spreads about how useful these programs are, the more people will take advantage of them over time.

Action Ideas:

1. If your programs have a slow start, don't give up. It takes time to catch on. Commit to at least six months to a year of programming.

2. Ask attendees how you can make the sessions more valuable. Listen to and act on their ideas.

3. Encourage people to invite their colleagues to attend. Using word of mouth will help to get the numbers up.

Make it right.

An audience member shared that she was at a meeting where she was berated by the rest of her team for dropping the ball on the part of a project she was responsible for completing.

During a break, her supervisor pulled her aside and let her know that HE did not send her the documentation she needed. He not only apologized, but he took ownership of his mistake in front of the whole group when the meeting went back into session.

Did he diminish his stature with this employee and the rest of the team? NO! He elevated it. He built a level of trust and accountability and led by example as to what to do in this kind of situation.

When managers admit their mistakes, employees learn that leadership is serious about being honest, open, responsible and accountable. This mindset is fundamental to creating loyalty.

Action Ideas:

1. Admit your mistake immediately and without excuses. Take responsibility for what you did. The sooner you accept what happened, the sooner you can make it right.

2. Don't blame others. Criticizing employees in front of their peers will worsen the situation and cause distrust with your team.

3. Prepare yourself for the consequences. They may not be as bad as you think – on the other hand; they may be worse. Suck it up and accept the hand you're dealt.

Provide educational resources.

Many of your employees are looking for ways to be better tomorrow than they are today. Training is an essential part of professional development.

Have a resource library and train your employees how to use it. Assign a specific topic or book chapter to an employee that he or she can share at an upcoming meeting or training session. You will reinforce the learning by having your staff members teach their peers. Remember, many of your staff may not be used to reading nonfiction books, so educate them on the value of learning and sharing ideas - then teach them how to do it.

These are the four levels of competence:

- Unconscious incompetence: you don't know what you don't know. (You've never had to tie your shoe)

- Conscious incompetence: you are aware of what you don't know. (You don't know how to tie your shoe)

- Conscious competence: you know what to do, but you have to think about how to do it. (You know how to tie your shoe, but it still takes effort)

- Unconscious competence: you know the job so well you don't even have to think about it. (Tying your shoe takes no thought or effort)

By exposing your workers to novel concepts, fresh ideas and innovative ways of thinking, you will open them up to all kinds of possibilities that will enable them to succeed.

Maintain current programming.

Monitor your training program's effectiveness and close any gaps. Pay attention to industry trends and ask your staff what training would be of most benefit to them and why.

Don't necessarily stick to topics that are immediately relevant to your employee's current employment status and experience. By widening their horizons, you may open doors of opportunity for them that they may not have considered.

Also, make sure the information contained in training is accurate. For example, if you ever take a communication class and the instructor quotes the Albert Mehrabian study that shows that only 7% of our communication is verbal – RUN! That study was disproved years ago, even by Mehrabian himself, and yet trainers continue to teach it anyway.

Action steps:

1. Instead of sending one person at a time to training, invite a small group to go together. Not only will they have the same conversation, but they will also have others to hold them accountable to act on what they learned.

2. Follow up with your employees after a training program to see what they learned and how they are going to implement it. You reinforce their lessons by having them recount what they learned.

3. Have your employees share what they learned with the rest of your team. In doing so, you'll expand the knowledge base of your entire staff.

Expand your search for talent.

Because of the war for talent that is raging (and talent is winning), you cannot continue to mine the same fields to find employees. Competition for top talent has created a challenge for companies of all sizes and industries.

If you are having trouble finding your ideal candidates, you may have to try a different approach to recruiting. Step out of your comfort zone and expand your search criteria. Consider bringing on people who have the right personality fit and train them to your way of doing business.

Action ideas:

1. **Use independent contractors** - just make sure they meet the legal definition of an independent contractor. In this "try before you buy" mode, you'll see if the potential employee is a fit for your team. Then you can hire them on full-time.

2. **Hire entry-level employees**. Consider candidates who have the personality, the drive, and the desire to work for you and then train them. You'll deal with less baggage and can "mold" the employee to your way of working.

3. **Use remote employees**. Look for jobs that can be done off-site and hire remote workers to fill those positions. You'll keep your operational costs down, increase your pool of talent and increase the number of hours for employees to work.

Taking the chance to step outside of your comfort zone when hiring and expanding your options to widen your candidate pool might seem a bit difficult, but the quality of talent that you will attract will make it all worthwhile.

Offer formal education opportunities.

Give your employees tuition reimbursement and encourage them to complete their college degree or a certificate course. Although most employees appreciate any help they can get in paying for school, this benefit is especially popular with Millennials and Gen Z (the generation following Millennials).

According to a Fortune Magazine article on providing unlimited tuition reimbursement, a survey by EdAssist discovered that "if asked to choose between similar jobs, nearly 60% of respondents would pick the job with strong potential for professional development over one with regular pay raises. One in two millennials said they expected an employer's financial support in paying for further education."

Action Ideas:

1. Pay for employees to take classes towards their degree, whether or not the program has anything to do with his/her job. You, and they, may discover unknown skills and talents.

2. Share your career story with your team members so they can understand how you got to where you are in your career. Telling them of your own trials and tribulations may inspire them not to give up on their dreams.

3. Celebrate your employee's graduation with public acknowledgment and a party. They worked hard for their achievement and they deserve your recognition of their efforts.

Utilize YouTube videos for employee inspiration.

SnackNation, a snack delivery service, holds "Sensei Sessions" every Monday at noon. During these meetings, the CEO shares updates and then gives the staff the time to share some of the things they are passionate about with the rest of the team.

Topics during these sessions include "personal development, goal setting, nutrition, or productivity hacking, and almost all of them include a motivational video clip." Your employees are watching videos anyway, and with countless hours of new content being uploaded every minute online, having the chance to narrow down the selection of what to watch may be just the inspiration your team needs.

Action Ideas:

1. Choose a theme for the meeting and let your employees pick videos that align with that topic. Give a time limit, so you can either watch shorter videos, or the team members can share the most powerful segment.

2. Kick off each of your meetings with an inspirational or humorous video. It will set the tone for the rest of your time together.

3. Want to go beyond using other people's videos? Involve your employees in the creation of a YouTube video. Get all departments involved and have some fun with it. Who knows, it may go viral.

PART 5

In sickness and in health

"People want guidance, not rhetoric; they need to know what the plan of action is and how it will be implemented. They want to be given responsibility to help solve the problem and the authority to act on it." ~ Howard Schultz, Starbucks

Give power to the people.

When empowering frontline employees, managers may have more latitude than they realize. It's true. You don't always have the power to change pay, increase benefits or modify company policies on a whim, but you can empower your team members in a variety of ways.

Here are a few ideas:

1. **Communicate openly.** Keep your staff in the loop and let them know what's happening in the organization. Share both good news and bad news – and listen for feedback.

2. **Give employees a voice.** Create a safe environment for people to share when they see that something is amiss. At Toyota, if line worker sees a problem with a car, he/she has the power to stop the entire assembly line until the issue is fixed.

3. **Address tensions between tenured and newer employees.** Don't let complaints fester. Be open to innovative ideas that may come from your recent hires.

4. **Show support for career development.** If an employee is looking for ways to enhance his or her career, provide that individual with options and a plan for career development.

Empowerment creates connection, which leads to employees staying with you. Given the shrinking talent pool, staff retention is vital to the long-term success of your organization.

Offer a challenging yet supportive work environment.

When you give your employees challenging tasks, you boost their creativity, productivity, and overall profitability. Why not look for jobs that are currently being done by supervisors and assign them to subordinates who are ready and willing to take on the assignments. You will increase visibility at the lower ranks and potentially determine your future leaders.

By challenging your workers, you may uncover their hidden strengths. You gain the benefit of using current staff to fill upcoming leadership roles, making your succession planning more fruitful. Hiring from the outside has its share of challenges, so why not take advantage of your homegrown talent who knows your company inside and out.

Action Ideas:

1. Encourage friendly competition between departments to see how everyone can make your products/processes better.

2. Assign employees to manage projects that stretch their abilities and require them to learn something new.

3. Delegate without dumping. Give employees the authority to make the decisions they need to make to complete the task successfully.

Encourage prudent risks.

When you provide a safe environment for innovative thinking, you'll grow faster than companies who refuse to "fix what's not broken."

An excellent way to encourage risk is to use "Get Out of Jail Free" cards. Employees can use these if they want to try something that involves a risk. By handing out these cards, leaders demonstrate that they value risk-taking. They assure staff that they have their back if the worker needs them.

Think about it, some of your best money-saving/making ideas may come from sources you never considered. If something goes wrong, learn the lesson and move on.

In his Entrepreneur Magazine article, "3 Ways Companies Can Encourage Smart Risk Taking," Salim Ismail shares three action ideas:

1. **"Resist the urge to say no."** To protect your organization from risk aversion, adapt the "First Rule of Improve" and start with "yes and."

2. **"Never stop experimenting."** To join execution and innovation, put our own set of experimentation processes in place.

3. **"Reward insightful experiments."** When your team is operating within strategic, commercial, ethical and legal frameworks and they avoid re-creating old mistakes, celebrate the failures that their willingness to experiment created.

Add meaning to work.

Every worker has different motivations. If you look at Maslow's hierarchy of needs, you'll find that many hourly employees stay at the first two levels and merely meet their physiological and safety requirements. They don't strive for the higher levels (Love/belonging; Esteem; Self-Actualization) to reach their full potential, either at home or work.

Research done on hourly workers finds that three core values are essential in their lives: meaning, dignity, and self-determination. Understanding these insights is key to increasing engagement.

Meaning: They want to feel that their contribution is valuable to the organization.

Dignity: They want management to treat them with respect.

Self-determination: They want to have a sense of control and ownership in how they do their work.

How can you make sure your employees' core values are being met?

_____

_____

_____

_____

_____

_____

Ask employees to create new ways to complete tasks.

Assemble an employee "think tank" and assign them a specific problem. See how many ideas they can come up with to solve the issue. Challenge them from a low-budget or no-budget standpoint to encourage creativity.

When brainstorming ideas, make sure that the goals of the project are understood. The team members need to be able to measure the progress of their plan compared to what is currently in place. Employees should have control over achieving their goal. Finally, remember to include a reward when the team meets their goals.

To add even more fun to the process, have a recognition ceremony for the best ideas of the year. Come up with various categories of awards and several nominees in each group so you can open the envelope and announce the winner – just like your own "Idea Oscars."

Action Ideas:

1. Conduct mind-mapping sessions. You may look to provide "Mind Mapper" or similar software so employees can capture their thoughts and brainstorming ideas legibly.

2. Give members of each team the opportunity to present their concepts to leadership and get feedback on their ideas.

3. Let the team, and the rest of the company, know when you implement an employee's ideas and keep them in the loop for any fruitful results.

Create an Employee Experience Committee.

Empower your staff to explore the changes they would ideally like to see in the workplace. Assemble a team whose sole purpose is to explore ways to improve culture and engagement. Give team members access to management to share their findings.

We can learn from the US Department of Commerce, as they are looking to increase engagement with their Employee Engagement Team. The team's mission "is to create an environment that values and supports employee engagement and promotes a healthy organization by developing internal programs and events for employees."

Their vision: "We envision an organization composed of dedicated leaders and employees who are committed to organizational success and job satisfaction."

An Employee Experience Committee will:

1. Measure current levels of engagement.

2. Solicit ideas and feedback from employees on how to increase their involvement.

3. Put together a plan for resources needed.

4. Share findings with management.

5. Follow up, review, and revise as necessary.

* Note to management: Act on your employees' suggestions. Let your workers know who suggested each idea and how you implemented it.

Share the greater mission.

When you have a well-defined vision, it's easier to make sure your employees share your organizational values.

Getting the right people "on the bus" is critical to having a company culture that rocks. Take an honest look at the people you have working for you. Are they still a fit for your business, or have you outgrown them? Are the people in the company in the right position or can you utilize their skill better elsewhere?

One example of a company that really defines its culture is Zappos. Check out their Ten Core Values:

- "Deliver WOW Through Service

- Embrace and Drive Change

- Create Fun and A Little Weirdness

- Be Adventurous, Creative, and Open-Minded

- Pursue Growth and Learning

- Build Open and Honest Relationships with Communication

- Build a Positive Team and Family Spirit

- Do More with Less

- Be Passionate and Determined

- Be Humble"

Circle your favorite(s). How will you implement them with your team?

Give back.

Millennial and Gen Z employees want to work for organizations that are serving a mission that is greater than themselves. Empower your employees to choose a cause(s) they'd like to support outside of the workplace. Then let them do it.

Back in the day, there were limited charities from which to choose. Now you'll find an agency for every type of need. There are apps for that! For example, CauseCast.com lets your employees choose the charities they most care about, so they are more likely to get involved.

By allowing employees occasional time off work to serve – once a quarter, twice a year, annually – whatever works best for your company – you'll invigorate your team with a renewed sense of purpose.

Action Ideas:

1. Want to know what charities are relevant to your workers? Ask!

2. Model the behavior you want to see. If you are asking your employees to give their time and volunteer, make sure you are doing the same.

3. Look for opportunities (Habitat for Humanity for example) that groups of employees can volunteer for at the same time. You'll build stronger relationships and friendships outside of the workplace.

Make your employees use their paid time off.

If you have employees who are proud of the fact that they "haven't taken a vacation in years," you need to change their attitude. It's not healthy nor helpful in the workplace.

There are way too many workers who don't use any or all their vacation time. They either think their manager will not allow the time off, or they're afraid that their coworkers will view them as slackers.

Vacations refresh and energize your team. In fact, employees usually get a lot of work done before leaving (the "Friday before vacation" syndrome). When and then they return to work, they are likely to come back with a renewed energy and an invigorated outlook.

Action Ideas:

1. Have a "Use It or Lose It" policy for at least part of your employees' vacation time. People want to save time for a special occasion, but often that "special time" never comes.

2. Take advantage of technology and let your employees work from home occasionally. Sometimes a change of scenery will give them a burst of inspiration.

3. Cross-train employees across departments so team members can easily fill in for their coworkers while they are on vacation. If you're still short of available workers, hire more people or bring in temps.

Build an employee-generated list of FAQs.

Because your employee handbook only goes so far in addressing everyday situations, let your employees help. Because they are on the front lines, serving your customers and working with each other, ask them to write down their most frequently asked questions (FAQs).

By using these kinds of real-world examples, you will be better equipped to define what works, and what doesn't work in your company culture.

Action Ideas:

1. Have a "Situation of the Week" contest. Address questions like "What did you do when an order got messed up?" or "What if a buyer wants something we can't deliver?" Share the answers so everyone can see the different ways of looking at these situations.

2. Pay attention to questions that you get from new employees. If you notice specific issues that come up on a regular basis, put together a procedure for handling them. This extra effort can help you in your customer service training as well as furthering your new hire onboarding process.

3. Compile the Q&A on your company intranet or newsletter. Recognize employees for their creativity in effectively handling questions and providing appropriate answers.

Discuss career development plans.

Regularly sit down the team members to define where they would like to be by the next checkpoint. Follow up on these conversations and help your employees achieve their goals.

Some terrific questions to ask your team members include, "What keeps you here?" "What can we do better to help?" and "What would cause you to leave?" The last two can be a little scary to ask, ask them anyway.

Research shows that companies that invest in their employees' career development reduce the risk of losing their most valuable employees to the competition. Plus, it's one of the things job applicants are putting a priority on receiving.

By providing an identifiable career path, along with coaching and mentoring for high potential employees, you are giving your staff what they need to move into new roles in your company.

Action Ideas:

1. Highlight employee success stories and share real-world examples of how to make progress through the organization

2. Encourage your managers to meet with their staff to find out the specifics of their career aspirations. Put together a specific plan to support them in achieving their objectives.

3. Make sure that each employee explicitly knows what they need to do to move to the next level. Do they need to take a certificate class? Finish their degree? Attend a training program? Tell them and give them the tools they need to succeed.

Demonstrate that you trust your people.

Allow workers to acquire what they need to do their jobs without having to jump through a lot of hoops to get it. Don't insist on approving every minute detail of a project. Trust that your employees have the experience, knowledge, and competence to handle a plan without constant oversight.

Managers who rule with an iron first – micromanaging, rigid control and negativity, create a climate of anxiety and fear. Although an autocratic management style may bring you a well-behaved workforce, it certainly won't encourage employees to bring up ideas or share potential problem areas. Give your staff the authority they need to act on their own.

Action ideas:

1. Delegate responsibilities. Give your employees full duties for executing a task or project. Hold them accountable for the results.

2. Convey clear expectations. Don't make your employees guess the desired outcome. Ask them what they believe they are supposed to do to achieve success.

3. Allow for flexibility in work schedules. Maybe permitting occasional telecommuting is an option. Does flex-time or job sharing make sense? Talk to your employees to find out what works best for them.

4. Banish unnecessary hierarchy. Give team members the latitude they need to approach management with their ideas and suggestions for better customer service.

Offer opportunities for job-sharing or cross-training.

With 10,000 Baby Boomers retiring every day, it's essential to have the workforce you need to get the job done. Cross-training not only adds depth and variety to your employees' skill level, but it also allows your management team to leverage the talent and expertise you already have in-house.

If you're finding your employees are disengaged, cross-training may re-ignite their spark and passion by giving them stimulating work to do. When you expose your staff to other jobs within the company, they feel a sense of growth and accomplishment while learning something new.

You can also use cross-training as a substitute for temporary workers. Your employees may travel between departments, while their understanding of the company's processes and value continues to expand.

Action Ideas:

1. Ask what they want. Let staff members identify the jobs they would like to learn and give them the chance to try it out. If an employee is struggling to answer, share your thoughts as to why you believe they'd be a good fit for a particular position.

2. Put together a program. A formal job rotation program provides everyone the opportunity to try something new.

3. Collect feedback. Ask employees what they like about the program and any areas they would improve.

Learn lessons from each failure.

In Liz Ryan's "Five Lessons Only Failure Can Teach You" article in Forbes Magazine, she shares these five lessons learned from making mistakes.

1. **"How to back up and reflect."** What went wrong and how can you prevent that from happening again?

2. **"How to fix something that breaks."** You now have a new skill and are better prepared for future events.

3. **"How to soften the energy."** When you stop being defensive and open up to yourself and others about what went wrong, you feel better.

4. **"How to set an intention."** Make a personal commitment to yourself to get the task done and realize that you may get distracted along the way.

5. **"How to make a mistake and keep going."** What doesn't kill you makes you stronger. Learn your lesson, let it go, and move on.

What is a lesson you've learned from a failure?

_____

_____

_____

_____

_____

_____

Acknowledge employee aspirations.

Account for both the personal and career interests of your employees. By focusing on the whole person and not just what they do at work, your organization will get more value from your team members.

For example, if an employee mentions that he or she has always enjoyed teaching, but they don't have any training responsibilities, look for ways to get them engaged in coaching or mentoring others. How do you find out what your employees' goals are? Ask them.

A textile manufacturing client went so far as to hire a dream manager to help connect their employees to their aspirations. This company supported their employees in creating a pie-baking business, a financial training program (that they also use in-house), and other business ventures. Give your employees time to process your sincerity in asking. They want to trust that you are taking them and their ideas seriously.

Action Ideas:

1. Ask your team members, "What can we do to help you achieve your goals?"

2. Encourage your employee to make a shared commitment to creating a win/win for them and your company.

3. Provide opportunities to let your employees share their newly developed skills within the organization.

Provide self-care opportunities for employees.

Chronic work-related stress is taking a toll on your employees' productivity. Research estimates that losses associated with stress cost US business $300 billion each year. What can you do?

Encourage self-care. When you help your employees make better lifestyle choices, you'll reduce your absenteeism, turnover, and health care costs, while boosting your throughput in the process.

Here are a few ideas to get you started:

Encourage Exercise. There are many physical and mental benefits to physical activity. Provide gym memberships or build a workout center. Give incentives to employees who walk, run, or bike to work instead of driving.

Promote healthy eating. If you're providing lunch or snacks during the day, bring in nutritious options. Holding a health fair will educate employees how to make better choices in what they eat.

Provide aid for quitting smoking. Because smoking reduces focus and concentration, it impairs productivity. Include a tobacco cessation program in your benefits. Your insurance rates may go down as well – bonus!

Support mindfulness practices. Hold yoga classes during lunch or offer stress reduction workshops throughout the month.

When you look at your employees holistically, your organization will benefit from a healthier, happier team.

PART 6

To love and to cherish

"Employees who believe that management is concerned about them as a whole person – not just an employee – are more productive, more satisfied, more fulfilled. Satisfied employees mean satisfied customers, which leads to profitability." – Anne M. Mulcahy

Go on an adventure

Getting out of the office for a company outing is an excellent opportunity to create an experience your employees will cherish for a long time. Because we spend our days cooped up indoors, an offsite retreat, camping or hiking expedition, or rafting adventure is a refreshing breath of fresh air - literally.

Look for activities that aren't too strenuous for the majority of your team, but that still provide an enjoyable obstacle to overcome. Research shows that when people work together to conquer a challenge, the connections built become ironclad.

Ask your team what they like to do and some they want to visit. Consider various skill levels - you need an activity that isn't too hard for beginners, but still presents a challenge for a more experienced participant.

Action Ideas:

1. Take advantage of seasonal activities. Consider some of the parks and recreational areas that are in your local area. You don't have to travel far to get a nice bang for your buck.

2. Set up a scavenger hunt in your city so teams of employees will not only get to hang out with each other, they will learn more about the place they live in the process.

3. Offer activities both during work hours as well as after-hours to get a higher level of participation across departments and shifts.

When they come back to work, your team will be energized, focused, and may have even made a few friends along the way.

Offer an employee wellness plan

Although many companies don't have the time, resources, or physical space to put a full gym, they can still encourage their staff to get up and do something active. Research shows that when employees are active for at least thirty minutes per day, their productivity increases by fifteen percent. Not only will you get more work done, but there's also a good chance your insurance premiums may decrease as well.

Exercise is one thing for optimal health; diet is another. According to one survey, sixty percent of employees feel more valued when they have a free lunch program. Like exercise programs, free food increases employee morale as well.

Action Ideas:

1. Measure off routes, and create a lunchtime walking goal for your employees. Put together a "mileage chart" to inspire employees to get involved as an individual or part of a team.

2. Have healthy snacks delivered. There are many delivery companies that not only bring in food, but they provide nutritional and background information about what the employees are eating.

3. Provide pedometers or have your employees download the same app to keep track of their progress. Give prizes when employees reach certain milestones.

When you consider that a healthy team is often a more productive one, doesn't it make sense to try to capitalize on such a crucial element of employee engagement?

Welcome new hires with flair.

Put together a welcome committee to enthusiastically greet new hires. Provide a company tour, a company-branded gift basket, and a welcome packet filled with information about groups, activities and local things to go.

Your welcome committee may consist of staff from different departments and shifts. The benefit for committee members is that they get a nice break from their routine. It also connects your new and tenured employees from day one.

Give new hires a VIP badge to show that they are a valuable addition to your organization. Assign a lunch buddy so they don't have to eat alone.

Remember, your new employee went on several interviews before accepting your position. Don't make it easy for another company to woo them away. Create an experience that makes them want to stay.

Action Ideas:

1. Start welcoming the new hire before their first day on the job. Start keeping in touch as soon as the offer is made and accepted.

2. Send a handwritten note, letting the new person know that you are looking forward to working with them. Have everyone in their department sign the card.

3. Put together an org chart with fellow team members' pictures on it so they can get familiar with the people they will be working with more quickly.

Understand personality styles.

Personality assessments are great tools to help staff understand each other better, and their use may improve the communication process. DISC is one of the more popular assessments, but there are numerous tests available.

Managers don't necessarily have to agree with, or even like some of their employees, but they MUST be respectful. It is the leader's job to figure out how to work most effectively with their team - no matter how their personalities are "wired."

To get the process started, have everyone take an assessment. Follow up with discussions or team building activities that allow different groups to learn about each other. When employees understand themselves and their colleagues, it creates more harmony. When it comes to employee engagement, it's not about "treating others the way YOU like to be treated," but rather it is about treating others "the way THEY want to be treated."

Reasons to incorporate personality assessments:

1. Employees have a better understanding of themselves and how to relate to each other.

2. You are more likely to get the right person in the proper position based on their style, attitude, and aptitude.

3. You'll create a more balanced team. Having all four personality styles on a team brings different perspectives and approaches to problem-solving.

Implement a leadership outreach program.

Find out what's happening in your company by scheduling face time with your employees. Caution: before starting, let your employees know what you're doing and why you're doing it. Tell your staff that you value their input and that you will be scheduling conversations with each of them.

If you don't pre-call your intentions, employees may be suspicious or think that they are in trouble. Keep in mind that the first couple employees who you invite for a sit-down may be wary of telling you the truth. Create an environment of trust so that, no matter what they say, you take it at face value.

Remember, their perspective is their reality. No, your workers probably don't know the whole story. No, your staff doesn't understand your situation and what you're going through, listen to what they have to say.

The only thing that matters is that you create a safe place for your employees to share, in their view, what is already working and what you can do to improve the company.

How can I create connections with my employees?

_____

_____

_____

_____

_____

_____

Encourage peer-to-peer recognition.

You know how important it is to show your workers how much you value them. But, receiving kudos from a coworker goes a long way in creating a highly-engaged workforce.

By focusing on peer-to-peer recognition, you create an accountability system. Employees can be free to look for ways they can help each other without feeling that they are "sucking up" to management.

Peer to peer recognition also helps in performance appraisals because employees soon learn that they can't act one way in front of their managers and another way in front of their peers.

Make the recognition fun, low-cost, and abundant. Don't limit employees' opportunities to recognize and appreciate each other. The more, the better!

Action Ideas:

1. Get the word out. Let your employees know who you are recognizing and why you are doing it. Give staff a chance to understand and support the kudos.

2. Be consistent. Make sure that employees know when and where they can expect to learn about the accomplishments of others – meetings, company newsletter, intranet, etc.

3. Be creative. Empower your team members to recognize each other in diverse ways to keep it interesting.

Start an employee referral program.

Encourage your staff to provide recommendations to fill open positions. You will get better hires when your employees refer people they know, like, and trust.

One general manager shared that he encourages his staff to post job openings on their personal Facebook pages. This strategy works because it is usually their best team members who are doing the sharing. These people are excited about working there, and their feelings are apparent in their posts. Gallup research shows that highly engagement people have a "best friend" at work, so it's in your company's interest to let those friendships happen.

Why let your employees recommend potential hires?

1. **Increase engagement and productivity.** The chances are good that if workers like their job, they are committed and productive. Therefore, they are more likely to recommend others who they know will be a good fit.

2. **Reduce recruiting costs.** Instead of spending all of your budget on traditional methods, offer your employees a referral fee. The amount should be modest, but worth the effort, and should be paid after the recommended employee has been on the job for a certain amount of time.

3. **Expands the diversity of the candidate pool.** The more employees you involve in your recruiting process, the more options you'll have to choose the most suitable talent for your open positions.

Establish a "buddy system."

Encourage your seasoned employees to mentor your newer staff members. You will benefit by retaining the knowledge and experience of your tenured employees and help them to feel relevant. The new hires will learn from someone who has been in the trenches and knows how to do the job.

Mentorship is a terrific way to create connections between the different generations in the workplace, thus enhancing your succession planning efforts.

Make sure you're teaming up people who are compatible and be okay if the first pairing doesn't work out. The goal is to create relationships and friendships on the job, thereby engaging both your new and your long-term staff members by letting them bond with each other.

Action Ideas:

1. **Train your mentors.** Don't assume that your employees know the attributes of a successful mentor. Let them know what their role encompasses and how to set boundaries with their mentees.

2. **Set up a time frame.** Establish a timeline of goals, the length of the commitment required, and a minimum number of meetings that the mentor and mentee will have.

3. **Measure success.** Look for increased job satisfaction and reduced turnover as evidence of a successful mentoring program.

Share the personal side of life.

Highly engaged management teams recognize that their staff is likely to be more engaged and productive when they bring their authentic selves to work. Allowing employees to share portions of their personal life creates a solid basis for connection.

When you offer opportunities for your staff to know each other personally AND professionally, you allow relationships to form. These work friendships help in increasing retention and reducing disengagement.

Action Ideas:

1. You may already have a "Bring your child to work day," why not try a "Bring your pet" to work day. As long as pets are well behaved, your employees and their pets may enjoy the extra time together. If bringing live pets to work isn't an option, a pet photo wall can also be a conversation starter.

2. Have a periodic "Show and Tell" where employees bring in something from home and tell their colleagues about it. As they share their hobbies, awards, collections, and other interests, you'll encourage people to connect based on mutual interests.

3. Give employees the opportunity to share a particular cause or charity they support. Allow them to post information on their favorite charity so your team can become better educated on the many causes they may choose to help.

Hold friendly competitions.

There are many ways to get employees involved in friendly contests. Host a variety of events, so you can get many of the staff involved as possible in the things they like best.

Pinterest.com has lots of ideas that you can use. With the number of "Pinterest Fail" sites, you can offer prizes for the best representation of a Pinterest idea as well as the funniest "fail."

Host a chili or BBQ cook-off or a brownie bake-off. Make sure the entries are anonymous, so it's fair for everyone. Encourage participants to bring in their "secret sauce" recipe and let the judging begin.

Here are a few benefits that friendly competition can bring to your workplace:

1. **A common goal.** Instead of focusing on individual achievement, a team goal takes everyone's ideas and opinions into consideration.

2. **Accountability:** Give everyone a role to play in achieving their teams' goals. Focus on the strengths of each player.

3. **Motivation and support.** Team members can encourage and cheer each other on to success.

4. **Breaks the monotony:** friendly competition can be a fun, and rewarding activity that shakes up the day and creates a buzz in the office.

Don't forget the prize or reward. To stay motivated and on track, offering a reward or prize is a great idea. Be creative with this! You don't have to spend a lot of money - nor should you.

Allow employees to switch jobs with each other.

When employees know, and are comfortable with each other's jobs, it helps them be more productive and efficient workers. You aren't dependent on any one employee to do a job, so it makes scheduling easier as well. It's important to keep the lines of communication open between workers and managers to ensure that there is adequate coverage to get the work done.

By fostering a culture of collaboration, your team will learn how they are all working toward a common goal. When employees take pride in being able to do their job as well as the job of others, they feel a greater sense of accomplishment in their ability. They will live up to the standards that you set for them and create the type of culture you want.

Action Ideas:

1. Ask for team members to volunteer to take on additional roles, so you develop a well-rounded, confident staff.

2. Minimize confusion by managing any position changes. Encourage open and honest feedback about your staff's needs and desires in each job they take on.

3. Provide formal training to your team members, so you know they are doing the job correctly, and are not inheriting the bad habits of coworkers in their established roles.

Cross training is a great tool that can be used in almost any position and in nearly every industry.

Use Icebreakers to get to know your team.

The Gallup Q12 is a list of statements that organizations can use to determine if their employees are engaged. One of the declarations is "I have a best friend at work." Icebreaking activities are a great way to help employees get to know each other personally and let the friendships begin.

You read earlier in this book about "Two Truths and a Lie." Here are a few more icebreakers to try:

1. **My Three Shining Moments** – Each person shares three significant moments from their life. These events may be personal or professional. Debrief it by finding the common threads in the highlights mentioned.

2. **My Favorite Things** – Pick a general topic (movies, TV shows, music) and have participants share what their favorite thing is and why. Debrief it by having people share what they learned about each other.

3. **Five of Anything** – Have attendees brainstorm five ideas about the meeting topic. For example, if you're meeting to discuss employee retention, have members come up with five things that cause them to stay at their job.

Creativity is encouraged, but keep it rated "G." Icebreakers help you learn things about others that don't come up in regular workplace conversation, thereby creating additional opportunities to connect.

Create a meaningful mission statement.

Does your company mission statement sound more like this: "Our primary objective is to maximize long-term stockholder value while adhering to the laws of the jurisdictions in which it operates and at all times observing the highest ethical standards."

Or like this: "Our mission: to inspire and nurture the human spirit — one person, one cup and one neighborhood at a time." (Starbucks Coffee)?"

Which statement do you think lets your employees know how their efforts make a difference in the greater mission and serve their customers, their communities, and, ultimately, the world?

If your organization's mission statement does not espouse values being lived by your team every day, it's time to create one that does. Ask for feedback from your employees so you can create a message that resonates with them all.

1. What do we do? Beyond your product or service, determine a common theme that inspires your employees to rally around it.

2. Why do you do it? Aside from making money, what is the ultimate reason you are in business?

3. Who do you do it for? Think about the ultimate impact your company has on your employees, their family, your customers, the environment, etc.

Once you answer those three questions, develop a short, repeatable statement that brings a collective sense of pride, mission, and purpose when repeated.

'Til Death Do Us Part?

Probably not. But by using the tips in this book, you'll increase the likelihood of your employees staying engaged, committed and dedicated to your company.

Keep the honeymoon going!

About the Author

Lisa Ryan is the Chief Appreciation Strategist at Grategy. She helps organizations keep their top talent and best customers from becoming someone else's through her engaging, interactive, and fun keynotes, workshops, and consulting assignments.

Grategy® programs focus on employee productivity and retention, customer loyalty, and overall growth. She is the author of nine other books and co-stars in two films, including the award-winning "The Keeper of the Keys" and "The Gratitude Experiment."

In addition to Grategy®, Lisa Ryan is a Regional Director with Leadership USA Cleveland. Leadership USA (www.LeadershipUSA.biz) is a membership organization that offers high-quality education for leaders of our member companies, via a monthly learning event with world-class instructors, who present on diverse topics.

Bring Lisa to your next event:

www.Grategy.com

lisa@grategy.com

216-359-1134.

Bibliography

12 Truly Inspirational Company Vision and Mission Statement
Examples. Lindsay Kolowich.
https://blog.hubspot.com/marketing/inspiring-company-
mission-statements

49 Employee Engagement Ideas (The Ultimate Cheat Sheet Your
Team Will Love), Tim Eisenhauer.
https://axerosolutions.com/blogs/timeisenhauer/pulse/206/
49-employee-engagement-ideas-the-ultimate-cheat-sheet-
your-team-will-love

Careers, Jobs, Employees, HR Practitioners, Benefits, Leave,
SES, Training, Human Capital. U.S. Department of
Commerce, Office of the Secretary, Office of Human
Resources Management.
http://hr.commerce.gov/AboutOHRM/PROD01_009669

Five Lessons Only Failure Can Teach You. Liz Ryan.
https://www.forbes.com/sites/lizryan/2015/12/29/five-
lessons-only-failure-can-teach-you/2/#6c8162cc39d5

Here are the Twelve Most Pet-Friendly Companies. Kia
Kokalitcheva. http://fortune.com/2016/03/08/here-are-the-
12-most-pet-friendly-companies/

How to Have an Effective Morning 'Ops' Meeting. http://www.forconstructionpros.com/construction-technology/personnel-management/article/10302249/how-to-have-an-effective-morning-ops-meeting

How to Increase the Motivation of Factory Workers. Andreas Slotosch. https://beekeeper.io/how-to-increase-the-motivation-of-factory-workers/

How to Select the Employee of the Month. Paula Clapon. http://www.gethppy.com/employeerecognition/select-employee-of-the-month

Please Micromanage Me, Said No Employee Ever. Lauren Lee Anderson. https://www.15five.com/blog/please-micromanage-me-said-no-employee-ever/

Remember to say thank you. Dr.Laura Trice.TED.com. https://www.ted.com/talks/laura_trice_suggests_we_all_say_thank_you

Talent Management in Manufacturing: The Need for a Fresh Approach. PWC.com white paper. https://www.pwc.com/gx/en/industrial-manufacturing/publications/assets/pwc-talent-management.pdf

The Advantages of Promotion from Within, Beth Greenwood. http://work.chron.com/advantages-promotion-within-6320.html

The Importance of Stay Interviews. HR Matters. https://www.hri-online.com/blog/the-importance-of-stay-interviews

The Power of Positivity, In Moderation: The Losada Ratio. http://happierhuman.com/losada-ratio/

The Triple Bottom Line: Measuring Your Organization's Wider Impact. https://www.mindtools.com/pages/article/newSTR_79.htm

These 6 Companies Give Their Employees Unlimited Tuition Reimbursement. Claire Zillman. http://fortune.com/2016/03/04/companies-employees-tuition-reimbursement/

Top Complaints from Employees About Their Leaders. Lou Solomon. https://hbr.org/2015/06/the-top-complaints-from-employees-about-their-leaders

Why 2016 is the Year for Veterans in the Workplace. Justin Constantine. http://www.industryweek.com/workforce/why-2016-year-veterans-workplace

Why Promoting from Within Usually Beats Hiring From
Outside. Susan Adams.
http://www.forbes.com/sites/susanadams/2012/04/05/why
-promoting-from-within-usually-beats-hiring-from-
outside/#75331bea3fb2

Why Should Companies and Employees Have Shared Values.
Scott MacFarland. http://www.huffingtonpost.com/scott-
macfarland/why-should-companies-and- b 4225199.html

Order *To Have and To Hold* for your next conference, workshop, retreat, or training program where you need ideas and strategies to jumpstart your engagement initiative.

Quantity pricing for direct purchase of the book. All discounts are savings from the retail price of $19.97.

25-100	$15.00 each
101-250	$14.00 each
250-499	$12.00 each
500 +	$10.00 each

Prices do not include shipping and handling.

Call for a complete pricing proposal or an estimate to your location.

Call or email: (216) 359-1134 or lisa@grategy.com

Visit our website for all the latest news:

www.Grategy.com